Take Heed to Yourself
Essentials for Ministry from 1 Timothy 4:16

Andrew D. Erwin

ISBN: 978-1-960858-90-0

Published by:

Cobb Publishing
704 E. Main St.
Charleston, AR 72933

(479) 747-8372
www.CobbPublishing.com
CobbPublishing@gmail.com

Dedicated to

Mike Kiser

A faithful gospel preacher and friend.

Table of Contents

Introduction

In this volume we have presented to the reader a study of 1 Timothy 4:16 – "Take heed to yourself and to the doctrine. Continue in them, for in doing this you will save both yourself and those who hear you." The chapters of this study are divided accordingly: (1) Take Heed to Yourself; (2) Take Heed to the Doctrine; (3) Those Who Hear You.

The reader will also observe that many of the sources cited in this volume are more than 100 years old. We would like to cite more recent works more often, but in the opinion of the author, nothing has surpassed the quality, the veracity, and the relevance of the books we have selected.

Undertaking such a book pertaining to preachers, preaching, and ministry is challenging for any preacher, "for who is sufficient for these things," especially this author. Yet feeling compelled to share with a wider audience the material offered in various workshops for preachers conducted by the author, in various places around the world, the present volume is placed before you with the hope that good will come from this effort. We will leave the usefulness of the content to the reader's discretion as we submit it to the praise and glory of Him who called us out of darkness and into His marvelous light.

ANDY ERWIN

Take Heed to Yourself - 1 Timothy 4:16

The Christian ministry cannot be entered like a common profession. As with Moses, Jeremiah, and Paul, the spirit of a reformer only lives within those preachers who minister from a place of necessity, and they cannot do otherwise. The desire to help and render everlasting good to his fellowman in the service of God must motivate the preacher, if he is to be effective and faithful in his work.

One's reason for entering ministry is more important than any natural abilities or giftedness he may possess. The motivation of the minister will eventually determine the efficacy of the ministry. In this way, the ministry of the word is to be distinguished from other fields of labor; and in this way, it is akin to other fields of service. The ministry of the word is "a service industry." Our Lord set the example by assuring His disciples that He came not to be ministered unto, but to minister and to give His life as a ransom for many. Moreover, He made clear that true greatness in His kingdom comes through service and ministry to others (Mark 10:43-45).

Why Do You Want to Preach?

Why is it that a man decides to preach? We might ask the same of a nurse, wondering "Why is it you have decided to be a nurse?" If the nurse says her decision was made for the money, flexible hours, and benefits, it might cause us to question her sincerity in caring for us when needed. If she says she was motivated by compassion for the sick and a desire to help those in need, her answer will likely put our hearts at ease. The same is true regarding preachers. Were we to ask a minister, "Why have you decided to preach?" and he were to explain that his decision to preach was motivated by pay, leisurely work, and comfortable hours, in time, he will come to be nothing more than an unfortunate blight on any congregation who upholds him.

If, on the other hand, the preacher provides motivations that are truly spiritual in nature, the church will be much more likely to have found a faithful gospel preacher. The man who is motivated by his love for the Lord, His word, and His kingdom is a man who has had the seed of ministry planted in His heart by God. The man who desires to save souls and please God will see his ministry grow and fruit will be produced from his relationship with his heavenly Father and his desire to honor Him. Such a minister is not a man who chose to preach as a profession, as a man might decide to become a banker, lawyer, or accountant. Preaching chose him. More specifically, God chose him.

The minister we are describing is someone who has had his heart broken by sin and healed by the cross. The message of hope and divine redemption lives and springs forth from his soul. He cannot help but preach. He is compelled – "Woe unto me if I preach not the gospel!" His motivation is blameless. He is willing to "spend and be spent" because of love – love for God, His Son, His church, His word, and the souls of men.

The kind of preacher we are describing is focused on a certain set of goals which produce fruit of everlasting significance. He lives to keep the mission of Christ alive. He yearns to save souls. Heavenly joy is brought to his heart when he sees the church growing. Truly, he hopes to help others realize the change of life that he has experienced and is experiencing daily. In so doing, he seeks to bring glory to God in word and deed through his ministry.

Many preachers may aspire most "to make a name for themselves," taking only the best paying churches with the easiest hours. They strive to become professional pulpiteers. In the spirit of patterning our ministry after the first century church, we must be ready always to do the work we are called to do at any hour. The gospel preacher will be called to make sacrifices of his time, his money, and his energy. If he is fully supported in his ministry by the brethren, he is blessed. If he receives no monetary compensation, he preaches just the same. His inheritance awaits him whether he is compensated fairly or not in this life.

The great preachers of the Restoration Movement sacrificed much for the cause of Christ. Their families did too. They went without many physical comforts so mankind might have spiritual blessings in Christ. The church grew because of their perseverance and sacrifices. These men were crucified to the world and the world to them. If a revival of biblical preaching is to occur in the pulpits of the Lord's church, it will be led by men who have consecrated themselves to God and have devoted themselves to laboring together with Him and others of like precious faith for the greatest possible good – the salvation of the world.

Sincere heavenly goals stemming from the heart of a genuinely spiritual man will produce a truly honorable ministry. However, even chosen vessels must be shaped by the Potter's hand. Each of the apostles was selected personally by Christ. Being chosen for ministry did not exclude the necessary preparation for it. Three years were spent preparing the apostles, and still more work was needed.

Peter and John were outstanding evangelists in Jerusalem when the church began. The pair was devoted to speaking those things they had "seen and heard" and worked to "fill Jerusalem" with their teaching. Though threatened, "they did not cease teaching and preaching Jesus the Christ." As a result, "the disciples multiplied greatly in Jerusalem, and a great many of the priests were obedient to the faith" (Acts 6:7).

Would these men have accomplished such great things for the Lord had they not first been prepared? What if John's pride and desire to be great in the kingdom had not been corrected? Would he have been satisfied to allow Peter to take a prominent role in their preaching ministry? What if Peter's cowardice had not been overcome? Would he have looked steadfastly into the eyes of the Sanhedrin and with a straightened backbone said, "We ought to obey God rather than men"? What would have become of these men had they not been properly prepared for ministry?

Sometimes a preacher's ministry appears to be nothing more than a little "wood, hay, and straw," loosely constructed upon the foundation laid by Christ, and he suffers loss when it is tried by fire. The pain endured through a failing ministry only helps to emphasize the need to be prepared for the work of an evangelist. A minister's life will be filled with triumphs and tragedies and every preacher must "take heed unto himself" so that his heart, soul, mind, and body can endure the inevitable trials and temptations, avoid the pitfalls, and contribute something of lasting significance to the kingdom of God. If we are to have faithful gospel preachers possessing a servant's heart, they must be prepared, molded, and refined by the hand of God.

The Preacher and God

Essentially, in the preparation of the minister, we are seeking to discover the answer to the question, "What qualifies a man to preach?" Is it education that qualifies him? Is it his age, marital status, or the size of his family? What of his natural abilities, the power of his voice, and the strength of his mind? Do these qualify him to preach? Do years of experience qualify a man to preach? Does his appearance, looks, and mannerisms disqualify him from being a gospel preacher?

When perusing the classified ads for churches looking for ministers, one might get the idea that these are the qualifications for a preacher. Yet, none of these things truly qualify a man to preach or to aspire to become a preacher. There is only one qualification for a man to become a gospel preacher – his personal relationship with God. "Other foundation can no man lay" for a life in ministry than the preacher's relationship with God. No amount of education or experience can conceal a preacher's poor relationship with God. Before he can ever begin to help others reconcile their relationship with God, he must first be reconciled. Otherwise, the blind will be leading the blind. Any leader in the Lord's church, whether he is an elder, a deacon, or a minister, must first take heed to himself and must continue this path, avoiding all the devil's pitfalls along the way.

In the ministry of the word, the first soul to be changed and saved is that of the preacher. *"Take heed to yourself"* and *"save yourself"* – this is the beginning of Paul's exhortation to Timothy. The preacher must exemplify the change he hopes to see in others. His relationship with God must be consecrated if he is to help others know the possibility of such a life. In fact, we can go as far to say, a preacher must be seeking life as it is truly meant to be lived, if he is to inspire others about the possibility of their living that life as well. "The things you have learned and received, heard and saw in me, do," this must be the goal in life to the faithful minister of the gospel.

A closeness must exist between the preacher and God. God becomes sanctified in the heart of the preacher. His words flow and his ministry exists because of his relationship with God. He is genuine. He is real. He is truly an ambassador for Christ. He is pleading with souls on Christ's behalf to be reconciled to God.

But "who is sufficient for these things?" (2 Corinthians 2:16) Preachers are human. They too are earthen vessels, weak, frail, and prone to err. Paul again provides the answer, "our sufficiency is from God, who also made us sufficient as minsters of the new covenant" (2 Corinthians 3:5, 6). Only God can qualify such men. Only can a man's love for God qualify him in the eyes first of himself and then of the world. Only with a trusting, faithful relationship with God set as a foundation for ministry, can the preacher rightly be called a "man of God," and only a man of God will fulfill this calling.

A Man of God

Men of God can be found throughout the Bible. Each time one is found, he is characterized most by his relationship with God. Abraham was a "friend of God." Noah was a preacher of righteousness who found grace in the eyes of God because he "walked with God." The Lord spoke to Moses "face to face, as a man speaks to his friend." David was a man "after God's own heart." Jeremiah was known by God before he was born. Daniel was "greatly beloved" of God. Ezekiel was trusted as a watchman over the Jewish people in captivity.

Each of these men knew they were sent by God, worked for God, and answered to God. The supreme example of Jesus for the preacher is to be about his Father's business, to do the works of Him who sent him, and to preach His word without reservation. "Not my will, but Thy will be done" must be in the heart of every preacher who seeks to be a man of God.

Yet, it is true that some sinners and saints alike will not always understand the devotion a preacher has to do the will of God and to speak the word of God. Sometimes preaching the truth will cause the preacher to have enemies. Sometimes these enemies "arise from among your own selves." Sometimes a preacher becomes an enemy for preaching the truth (Galatians 4:16). He must remain a servant of the Lord, rather than men. If he chooses to serve men, he cannot be the servant of Christ (Galatians 1:10).

Only if the preacher's relationship with God is most valued, will he preach "in season and out of season." A preacher certainly must love his brethren and the souls of men, but he must love God *more*. Paul, like Ezekiel, was "free from the blood of all men" because he did not hesitate to preach the whole counsel of God.

The great temptation the "professional" preacher faces is that of compromise. If he is content to speak to the brethren those "smooth things" that some want to hear, and to tickle their ears with fables, then their blood will be on his hands. If job security is more important to him than the eternal security of the souls entrusted to his teaching, he will have to answer to God.

Considering the stricter judgment a preacher will face, James admonishes "be not many teachers." It is unfortunate that some brethren will hold a preacher's livelihood over his head and dismiss him for preaching the whole counsel of God, but even such heart-wrenching events can be endured through steadfast love of the Lord. Even if everyone in his care forsakes him, the faithful gospel preacher remains in the trusted care and kind providence of the Almighty God.

Preachers must, therefore, guard their relationship with God. The man of God must treasure his relationship with God. "Keep your heart with all diligence!" Even in much fear and trembling, the faithful steward of the word can trust in God and His immeasurable grace to provide strength and comfort in times of need, despair, and distress.

The Preacher and Prayer

Prayer has the power to heal sickness and cure diseases – both spiritual and physical. Prayer needs practice, not proof. The preacher's understanding of prayer and devotion to it is a product – for better or worse – of his relationship with God. If the preacher ever questions his closeness to God, he needs only to reflect upon his practice of prayer. God is as close to the faithful minister as his next prayer. God will always be just as close to a person as that person wants Him to be. When a minster is feeling far from God, he must ask himself how much time he is spending with Him in prayer. We speak most often to those who are closest to us. It is not different with God. If one is truly close to God, he will speak often to his Father.

In despondencies and depressions, when preachers feel like they deserve Him the least, is when they need God the most. The preacher's relationship with his Father reminds him that he does not have to be perfect to be in the presence of God. Through prayer he is making known to the Father that he is choosing to live in God's strength rather than his weakness.

A preacher's prayer life should never consist of simply giving a "to do list" to God. Prayer is not about getting God ready to do man's will. Prayer should prepare man to do God's will. The prayers of the preacher are for his life and the life of his congregation. His deepest concerns can be poured out in earnest supplications before the Lord. He can beseech the God of all grace for "mercy and find grace to help in time of need."

When his family is under attack, let him pray. When his marriage is under attack, let him pray. When he believes he is failing in his work, let him pray. When lonely, pray. When helpless, pray. When bitter, pray. God knows when his servants are hurting. During these times of despair, the faithful minister will find that "the hand of the Lord is not shortened that He cannot save, nor is His ear dull that He cannot hear."

Again, when we look to the supreme example of Christ, we find that Jesus did not just teach about prayer, He lived through His prayers. The Gospels bear witness to the prayers of our Lord. He prayed privately. He prayed frequently. He prayed for the future of the church. He prayed when facing decisions. He prayed when tempted. Our Lord prayed when facing death. If Jesus needed to pray, how much more do preachers need to pray today? Jesus only had three years of public ministry, yet He was never so restricted by time that he could not spend hours in prayer. A man's ministry will never ascend to greater heights without prayer. In fact, his ministry will never go beyond his prayers.

The apostle Paul prayed for the churches, elders, and servants in the places where he had been. He prayed "without ceasing" (Colossians 1:9), "night and day" (1 Thessalonians 3:10), and "always" (Philippians 1:4). Regardless of the congregation, Paul knew the people and their specific needs. He desired for the church to be built and strengthened through knowledge and wisdom of God's plan. He prayed that churches would grow in their love for one another and all men. Paul prayed that lives would be fulfilled in Christ and that Christ would be glorified. Observe,

"And this I pray, that your love may abound still more and more in knowledge and all discernment, that you may approve the things that are excellent, that you may be sincere and without offense till the day of Christ, being filled with the fruits of righteousness which are by Jesus Christ, to the glory and praise of God" (Philippians 1:9-11).

A preacher of the gospel should desire God to be at the heart of his ministry, both blessing and sustaining the people he is seeking to save. Prayer seeks God's intervention not only on behalf of the preacher, but also on behalf of the flock.

Ministry without prayer is like a body without air. God will breathe the breath of life into one's ministry through prayer. When he fails to pray about life and ministry, the preacher is conceding (whether consciously or not) that God is not needed. Choosing not to include God through prayer is tantamount to believing that one is self-sufficient for that work. Choosing to pray faithfully, however, is admitting one's need for God and that sufficiency can only come from God.

If the preacher truly desires his ministry to be a ministry of reconciliation, prayer will be in his heart and at the heart of his ministry. The man of God cannot succeed without God! If the preacher's prayer life is weak, his ministry will be listless. He will not have because he has not asked. And the one who has, "to him more will be given, and he will have abundance; but whoever does not have, even what he has will be taken away from him" (Matthew 13:12).

A man of God must follow the maxim which states, "Talk to God about your flock before you talk to your flock about God." Go to God during sermon preparation. Go before the Lord concerning any problems in ministry. Seek the Father's will before making any decisions. Pray for guidance always. Pray that God will give heavenly wisdom, compassion, and love.

Seek His spiritual blessings through prayer. As God grants these spiritual blessings, the preacher will become more of a spiritual blessing to the church. Pray that God will use you to accomplish the greatest possible good, "according to the measure of the grace of God that is in you." Doors of opportunity will be opened that no man can shut. Souls will be saved, and the church will grow both spiritually and numerically.

Studying the Word of God

Being prepared to preach the gospel requires putting time into the study of the word. Only "those who by reason of use have their senses exercised to discern both good and evil." Discernment and the acquiring of knowledge takes time and work.

A professor once shared a story with our class about a time he was visiting with an older preacher. The professor was in awe of the man's knowledge and told him he would give twenty years of his life to know the Bible the way the older brother knew it. To which, the older preacher replied, "You'll give a lot more than that."

A preacher will not be able to reach his goals in ministry without study. The preparation of the preacher must include the ongoing study of the holy scriptures which are able to make him "wise unto salvation." He must grow in God's grace and knowledge if he is to help others do the same. The preacher must not be ignorant of the Lord's righteousness revealed through the gospel if he truly desires to see his people to submit to the righteousness of God.

The man who is preparing himself for a life of ministry must place realistic expectations upon his level of knowledge in the word of God, especially at the beginning of his ministry. The church and their elders must do the same. It is unfair to expect a preacher who is twenty-five years old to have the knowledge of a minister who has twenty-five years of experience. The preacher, like all Christians, must be permitted time to learn, to grow, and to increase in his understanding and wisdom.

Some men have the advantage of having known the holy scriptures from childhood. Others have not been so fortunate. However, this lack of training in one's upbringing can be overcome by a sincere love of the truth. The man who desires to learn and loves to study the scriptures will soon catch up and possibly exceed the knowledge possessed by men who are many years his senior in ministry.

Some preparation for ministry can be achieved by studying the word of God in-depth in various colleges, universities, and schools of preaching. But no academic program exists that will take the place of lifelong, dedicated, devoted study of the word of God. A student of the scriptures must never stop studying. Academic programs of study can serve to introduce a preacher to the text and the various scholars and theories in the field of theology; but there is no academic degree that will replace the years of study spent beyond the classroom.

The preacher must approach his lifelong study and accurate handling of the word of God with a workman's mentality. He should realize that he is not yet the preacher he can be and will be without more study. "He who knows he needs to know more, already knows what he needs to know most." A man who enters ministry without knowledge of the Bible is "unskilled in the word of righteousness" and he will remain that way unless he begins to study. Through study his senses will be exercised, and he will be able "to discern both good and evil." Only by studying the scriptures as the Bereans of old will the preacher be able to contend for the faith, convince the gainsayers, and awake those who are resting comfortably in their spiritual slumber.

Study of the scriptures will also increase a preacher's confidence in his sermon preparation and presentation. Knowledge is powerful. Power in the pulpit comes from the living and active power of God's word being transmitted through the preacher to the listener. Knowledge builds confidence. A great distinction can be heard in the sermons which originate from a place of thorough knowledge of the subject and those that do not. When a preacher is thoroughly convinced of his sermon's veracity, he will "speak as the oracles of God." Faith will come from hearing his message.

Thoughts will ascend on high, and listeners will be edified and encouraged to submit their respective wills to the will of God.

A Preacher's Library

The preacher today has greater access to a more substantial number books pertaining to biblical studies than at any point in the long history of man. The preacher must take advantage of this "five-talent" opportunity and not bury it in the sand. However, a preacher's library does not have to be vast to be valuable to his studies. It is better for a man to be thoroughly familiar with a small number of books than to be completely ignorant with an enormous collection of books.

Solomon correctly said, "Of making many books there is no end, and much study is wearisome to the flesh." The preacher must be judicious in his selection of books for his library. Not all books are valuable. He must learn to "eat the fish and throw the bones away." Such discipline requires work. Discernment of truth and error is significant to "the work of an evangelist" and the work can never be fulfilled without it.

Joe Blue was a great evangelist in the state of Arkansas. He carried only a few books with him in his saddle bags. A young preacher once wrote to him requesting some of his sermon outlines. Brother Blue mailed him a copy of the New Testament with a little note included which said, "I get all of my sermons from this book, and it is chock full of good material!"

Brother Blue was wise in his advice to the young preacher. Of all the books a preacher might have in his library, none will be more important to the work of the minister than the Bible. Many preachers have seen their effectiveness in teaching and preaching God's word "destroyed for a lack of knowledge." If we are to be preachers of the word, and take part in the ministry of the word, we must know the word.

Yet, anyone who has ever prepared and presented a sermon can sympathize with the young preacher's request. It is a daunting task and some guidelines for sermon preparation are needed along the way. Sermon books can be a valuable part of the preacher's library. He must avoid the pitfall of preaching another man's sermons verbatim, less he loses his own personality and natural giftedness in his presentation of the material. Sermon books can help with ideas, outlines, vocabulary, and grammar. Debate books can sharpen a preacher's discernment of truth, error, logic, and reason. Commentaries can also be used to gauge one's thinking about difficult texts. But, of all the books this preacher can recommend, three will prove to be most value – a good study Bible, an exhaustive concordance, and a Bible dictionary and/or encyclopedia.

The preacher's motivation for study testifies of his motivation for ministry. If his studies are stimulated by the notion of diplomas hanging on his office wall, for personal satisfaction, or for an increased reputation as a Bible scholar, he may eventually have these things; but the church will be little better for it. If, however, he desires to learn the word of God so that His word might live within him, so that he might overcome the wicked one, and so that he might help others to live victoriously in Christ, then his study will be of great and everlasting benefit to those that hear him. Souls will be saved, the saved will be edified, churches will grow, and God will be well pleased.

Time Management and Study

Ironically, the love of studying can become a pitfall to a preacher's ministry if it is not properly balanced with social interaction among his people. A man can become so "at home" in his library and so consumed his study that he leaves no time for the flock.

A preacher not only shares his study with the flock through sermons, articles, and classes, but also in conversation, visitation, and prayer. For example, a preacher's informed knowledge for comforting the sick and bereaving gained from thoughtful study of the book of Job is of little use to the flock if the sick and bereaved are never comforted personally. Knowledge is often most useful to others in distress when it is shared personally, thoughtfully, and sympathetically.

Preachers must work to "redeem the time." H. Leo Boles was a great preacher, author, and educator. He made a disciplined practice of reserving several uninterrupted hours a day for study. Students and frequent guests knew not to visit him during those hours of the day unless it was an emergency. They knew he would be studying the word! A preacher could do the same with calls and visits. Time and place must be given to personal evangelism as well. If time is managed properly, much good can be done in a routine workday.

Choosing Educators and Mentors

The education of a minister can be a blessing or a curse, depending on the educator. The man who is preparing to devote his life to preaching the gospel should first be educated in the fundamentals of faith. First principles are not to be spurned but *learned.* When fundamentals are not learned, a trickle-down of apostasy occurs. The preacher will inevitably teach error, whether he realizes it or not. In order to learn the fundamentals of Christianity, one needs first to be taught them. To be taught the fundamentals one must sit at the feet of teachers who are prepared and willing to teach them because they believe them.

Not all theological schools are teaching the fundamentals of the faith. For this reason, many preachers have been led astray when seeking degrees. The prestige of the degree is for some more valuable than the veracity of the education received. The aspiring preacher must be careful who he permits to become his teacher. "Evil communications corrupt good morals."

It is true that there are no perfect schools, or teachers, or students. We are all made of clay and filled with various weaknesses. Yet, the prospective student must remain judicious in his selection of would-be teachers. Does the preacher wish to be molded in the image and follow the steps of faithful men? If so, he must sit at the feet of faithful men.

A man may study at a denominational seminary and be taught denominational doctrines which challenge and ultimately change his view of biblical truth. He may attend a secular university where classes are taught in religion by atheists and agnostics. A man may also attend a school which is radically conservative, and a new breed of Pharisee is waiting teach him. Some teachers in theological schools are teaching a new hermeneutic, which yields to moral relativism and strays from any universal application of scripture. Hence, what is true for one person may not be true for another.

What has been deemed a new hermeneutic, therefore, must have a new homiletic, a new way of presenting scripture in sermons. Accordingly, preachers are advised not to offer applications and conclusions based upon the biblical truth taught in the sermon. Instead, they are told to preach in narratives and to leave the conclusion open-ended, or up to the hearer, so that everyone can decide what the text means personally. It matters little what the text means to God, but what it means to the individual is of utmost importance.

The man preparing to preach should beware that some teachers who have never truly been converted are sitting in the professor's chair in certain institutions of religious studies. How can he expect a man who despises the church to inspire a love for the church in the hearts of his students? How can he expect a man who does not actively seek to save souls to encourage his students to be soul winners? How can the would-be preacher expect someone who lacks respect for the authority of the Bible to train his students to respect "thus says the Lord"?

The preacher-student must carefully consider the principle of reproduction. Man does not produce, he reproduces. Man reproduces what he has become. What does the man wish to be in life and ministry? This is a question each man must answer before he decides who will be his teachers.

Schools can better assist men who are preparing to preach by offering more programs concentrating on practical theology in ministerial training and preparation. Much of the minister's educational experience is being filled with obscure academic topics rather than practical and essential lessons which will prove invaluable to his work.

Being a gospel preacher requires more than being academic. It is better to go to heaven with no degrees than to be lost for all eternity with many prestigious degrees which robbed the preacher of his trusting faith in Christ. A minister's education must be balanced with education in the classroom and in the field alongside faithful, tried, and true servants.

Churches, preachers, and preacher-students alike should consider utilizing the role of the ministerial apprentice. After the young man's course of study is completed in the classroom, or in conjunction with it, he should work alongside a good and godly man who has labored for many years. Let the older man teach the younger man. Such a relationship could be a blessing for both men if they have the right spirit and desire to work together.

One final matter should be discussed concerning the preacher and his education. This is the egregious practice of buying degrees. Such a "degree" is not worth the paper it is written on. A degree does not have to be regionally accredited or recognized by civil governments to be valuable and useful to a minister; but something must be learned, some work must be required. Otherwise, what has a man profited by acquiring the degree? What has he gained? If a man is truly preparing to preach, he must be prepared in part from the labor of his studies. The man who decides to purchase a fraudulent degree from a "degree mill" has deliberately cheated himself. He will be at a severe disadvantage in his work, erring, not knowing the scriptures. He will eventually be exposed as a fraud. A "doctor" without an education is malpractice in the medical field. It should be considered malpractice-plus in the Lord's church. An even worse consequence is that his capabilities, natural talent, and giftedness will go untapped and unharnessed through the rigors of a legitimate education because he has essentially decided to take the easy way.

No shortcut exists for learning the word of God. Much study is required, and a certain "weariness of the flesh" will be exacted. The preacher must think about his goals for life and ministry when determining his educational pathway. He must think about the dear souls who will sit at his feet.

The sacrifices made to procure a good education will be repaid later in life by the many doors the Lord will open for the preacher who painstakingly prepared himself the right way. He will be able to walk through those doors with his head held high, knowing that he is not there by chance, good fortune, or brotherhood politics, but by hard work, determination, and the providence of almighty God.

Ministry should not be perceived or idealized from a purely positive perspective. Preachers need to be aware of both the dos and don'ts that come with the life he has chosen to build for himself and his family.

Concerning Immorality

Im·mo·ral·i·ty – the state or quality of being immoral; wickedness.

Scripture is clear on matters of immorality and wickedness. One needs only to read the "works of the flesh" to find examples. The preacher must allow scripture, not personal scruples, or opinions "over doubtful things" to determine matters of morality. When everything is made out to be a matter of morality, the risk of nothing becoming a matter of morality increases.

A preacher can condemn every opinion which differs from his own, until no one takes his stance on moral issues seriously. He can major in minors to the point of everything seeming to be major to him, and thus everything seems to be minor to the audience. He becomes "the boy who cried wolf." When the wolf finally appears, no one listens.

In time, the preacher may even refuse to listen. A man can be stretched so far in one direction, that when he is released from Pharisaical opinions and ceases straining out the gnats, he will go too far to the left and develop more of a moral subjectivity rather than a biblical ethic. In these cases, his teaching will become weaker, and his own moral uprightness will be diminished.

History is full of preachers who ruined their influence for good by indulging in immorality. Sadly, some of these men were once blameless in doctrine and life. A few, however, were merely wearing a façade and their sins found them out.

One of the most notorious immoralities occurring among ministers is that of marital infidelity. The most effective way to avoid this pitfall is to stop it before it transpires. On one occasion, a fine gospel preacher was staying in the home of a Christian family while he was conducting a gospel meeting for their congregation. The husband left for work one morning. The preacher opened his door to the knocking of the wife and found her completely naked. Immediately, this good man fell to his knees and began praying for the women, her husband, and her family. When he opened his eyes, she was gone. Before falling to temptation, fall to your knees and pray!

Controversies have riddled the brotherhood in recent years through a barrage of sins such as homosexuality, pedophilia, drug addiction, thievery, spiritualism, the occult, and even atheism. How can this be? How could this happen to those who were supposed to be men of God? How can a preacher of the gospel come under the influence, impulse, and "sway of the wicked one"?

The danger of carnality exists for everyone, preachers included. Every Christian must make a daily commitment to discipline and train against evil. A battle is transpiring for the minds of men. The mind is the primary instrument with which man glorifies God. Success or failure, in life or ministry, depends on the mind of the individual.

Has the person been renewed in the spirit of his mind? Has he been transformed by the renewing of his mind? The carnal mind is at enmity with God and is not subject to the law of God. But the spiritual mind manifests life and peace in the believer. Let us commit ourselves to being "crucified with Christ" and "die daily" in service to the King as living sacrifices to God.

The preacher is on the front lines in the battle for the minds of men. He is seeking to change the world one soul at a time. The first soul which needs changing and constant renewal is his own. He must first "gird up the loins of his mind" if he is to lead others in this battle for greater spiritual mindedness. Moreover, the preacher must remember that he is stationed in a position to help those with a renewed mind to keep their faith when confronted by the wickedness of the world.

Our hope for any wayward preacher is that his sin does not become a "sin unto death." Our prayer is for his repentance and restoration to the body of Christ. While his weaknesses have brought disappointment to the kingdom of heaven, his returning can also be a cause for celebration. Let us labor to this end, "considering ourselves lest we also be tempted."

Management of Finances

A word should be said in the context of pitfalls in ministry about the preacher and his finances. The minister must support his family just as any man should. He should know what amount of salary is necessary to support his household and honestly discuss the matter with the church's leadership upon beginning the work. If the preacher does not receive adequate compensation in the beginning of the work, it is unlikely that he will ever receive it.

He must learn to make do and not live beyond his means. Like anyone else, the preacher should budget, avoid credit cards and high interest loans, and discipline himself to save for unexpected needs. It is good to enjoy a meal at a restaurant, for example. It makes for a nice treat on occasion. But if the preacher and his family frequent restaurants often, their money will be spent, and they will hardly know where it went.

Jack Meyer, Sr. offered the following critique: "Financial debt seems to be one of the most devasting plagues to preachers."[1] He gave three reasons why he believed undue debt occurred for preachers: (1) Poor management of income; (2) Exacting demands of the public; and (3) The natural desire to be liberal [charitable] with money.

Preachers live in glass houses. If a neighbor writes a bad check or is late on a payment, it may never be known. But if the preacher does so, the church and the community will be talking about him long after he has gone. Embarrassments like these can be avoided with frugality and budgeting.

Ministers should probably seek the advice and guidance of financial experts. When discussing financial management with experts, things like health insurance, taxes, and retirement funds should be considered and arrangements made.

Consider your spouse. Refrain from putting the brunt of the family's financial management on her shoulders. Be sure she is involved in key purchases and aware of the family's financial standing. Work together. Don't keep secrets, like credit cards. Use any financial flexibility you receive to "live joyfully with the wife who you love" (Ecclesiastes 9:9).

Physical and Mental Health

One of the great challenges a preacher will face is to give proper and adequate attention to the care of himself – physically and mentally.

Physical and mental health are not always mutually exclusive. In many ways the two are related. Proper diet, exercise, and rest

---

[1] Jack Meyer, Sr., *The Preacher and His Work* (Shreveport, LA: Lambert, 1960), 113-114.

can provide untold benefits to one's mental health as well as physical. "Because of the strenuous demands which are continuously made of the minister, he should be a man of robust health."[2] And, "one can only get robust sermons from a robust man."[3] Truly the minister must be sound in doctrine and in body lest his work be crippled with the fear of breaking down.[4]

While a preacher should not be expected to be a marathon runner or an Olympiad, "Physical considerations are not despicable"[5] and much good can be done for the body "by proper food, little enough of it, pure air, and sufficient exercise."[6] The preacher is to be a "man in physical life."[7] Much of true "manhood" has been lost in recent years. It appears, Paul's charge to "act like men" is as relevant as ever, especially for preachers. A manly presence in the pulpit and in the daily life of the church is to be admired and encouraged.

In his classic, *Lectures on Preaching*, Phillips Brooks urges preachers "to conquer the tyranny of his moods, and to be always ready for his work."[8] He warned preachers about self-indulgence, and only going to work when they feel like it. He cited Jesus as an example of a preacher who continued His work even in much weariness. Read closely Brooks' stirring charge to preachers:

---

[2] Batsell Barrett Baxter, *The Heart of the Yale Lectures* (New York: Macmillan, 1954), 91.

[3] Ian Maclaren, *The Cure of Souls* (New York: Hodder & Stoughton, 1896), 276.

[4] Ibid, 275-6.

[5] John Hall, *God's Word through Preaching* (Grand Rapids, MI: Baker, 1979), 82.

[6] Ibid.

[7] Arthur S. Hoyt, *The Preacher: His Person, Message, and Method* (New York: Hodder & Stoughton, 1909), 41.

[8] Phillips Brooks, *Lectures on Preaching* (New York: E.P. Dutton and Co., 1877), 65.

"It is part of the privilege of our humanity, it is part of the advantage of our people in having men and not machines for ministers, that we preach the truth in various lights, or shades, according as God brightens or darkens our own experience; but any mood which makes us unfit to preach at all, or really weakens our will to preach, is bad, and can be broken through. Then is the time for the conscience to bestir itself and for the man to be a man."[9]

In Charles Spurgeon's *Lectures to His Students* an entire chapter is dedicated specifically to "The Minister's Fainting Fits"[10] to address one of these moods which must be overcome – *melancholy*. Spurgeon was himself prone to bouts with depression and devoted this space to encourage ministers to persevere. He was not the first or the last preacher to battle depression and much of what he wrote came from his personal experience. Spurgeon began the lecture by noting, "Fits of depression come over most of us... The strong are not always vigorous, the wise not always ready, the brave not always courageous, and the joyous not always happy."

Spurgeon believed a minister may suffer depression for a few reasons, beginning with the fact that they are men and "Being men, they are compassed with infirmity, and heirs of sorrow." He continues, "Good men are promised tribulation in this world, and ministers may expect a larger share than others, that they may learn sympathy with the Lord's suffering people, and so may be fitting shepherds of an ailing flock." Seeing that, "We have the treasure of the Gospel in earthen vessels, if there be a flaw in the vessel here and there, let none wonder."

---

[9] Ibid, 66.
[10] Charles Spurgeon, *Spurgeon's Lectures to His Students*, ed. David Otis Fuller (Grand Rapids, MI: Zondervan, 1945), 132ff.

The famous preacher also cited poor physical health as another cause for a preacher's depression as "most of us are in some way or other unsound physically." He notes specifically digestive health and organs as being "the fruitful fountains of despondency." Fresh air and exercise are recommended. He believed, "Repose is as needful to the mind as sleep to the body." Thus, "Rest time is not waste time. It is economy to gather fresh strength." And "even beasts of burden must be turned out to grass occasionally." Spurgeon concludes, "It is wisdom to take occasional furlough."

The nature of the minister's work can also cause depression. "Our work, when earnestly undertaken, lays us open to attacks in the direction of depression. Who can bear the weight of souls without sometimes sinking to the dust?" Furthermore, "All mental work tends to weary and to depress, for much study is a weariness of the flesh; but ours is more than mental work – it is heart work, the labor of our inmost soul."

Moreover, "It is our duty and our privilege to exhaust our lives for Jesus. We are not to be living specimens of men in fine preservation, but living sacrifices, whose lot is to be consumed; we are to spend and be spent, not to lay ourselves up in lavender, and nurse our flesh."

The lack of human sympathy and loneliness is spoken of as "a fertile source of depression." Elijah, Jeremiah, and John the Baptist are considered examples of the onslaught of depression which occurs when the man of God is isolated from fraternal and kindred minds.

An interesting phenomenon occurs during the "hour of great success" as "The Lord seldom exposes His warriors to the perils of exultation over victory; He knows that few of them can endure such a test, and therefore dashes their cup with bitterness."

Spurgeon opined, "Poor human nature cannot bear such strains as heavenly triumphs bring to it; there must come a reaction. Excess of joy or excitement must be paid for by subsequent depressions...lest he boast himself beyond measure." Thus, the man of God is made to endure secret humiliation "to keep them in their proper place."

Contrariwise, "Before any great achievement, some measure of the same depression is very usual." Spurgeon believed such depression will come whenever the Lord is preparing His servant for a larger blessing in ministry. As a "prophet in rough clothing," such depression served as "the scouring of the vessel" to fit it for the Master's use. Thus, "Defeat prepares for victory."

Brethren can become a source of depression for the minister. Through betrayal, apostasy, harsh words of criticism, division, slander, foolish censures, and inadequate support, "the soul is hardened to the rough blows which are inevitable in our warfare; but at first these things utterly stagger us, and send us to our homes wrapped in a horror of great darkness."

"Constant dropping wears away stones, and the bravest minds feel the fret of repeated afflictions." Indeed, "The trials of a true minister are not few, and such as are caused by ungrateful professors [professing the faith] are harder to bear than the coarsest attacks of avowed enemies. Let no man who looks for ease of mind and seeks the quietude of life enter the ministry; if he does so he will flee from it in disgust."

Spurgeon also devoted some attention to what he deemed "causeless depression." He shared his struggle, stating, "One affords himself no pity when in this case, because it seems so unreasonable, and even sinful to be troubled without manifest cause; and yet troubled the man is, even in the very depths of his spirit." Continuing, he adds, "My witness is, that those who are honored of their Lord in public, have usually to endure a secret chastening, or to carry a peculiar cross, lest by any means they exalt themselves, and fall into the snare of the devil."

Spurgeon concluded by offering some remedies for depression. First, "The lesson of wisdom is, be not dismayed by soul-trouble. Count it no strange thing, but a part of ordinary ministerial experience…think not that all is over with your usefulness. Cast not away your confidence, for it hath great recompense of reward."

Secondly, "Cast the burden upon the Lord…Care more for a grain of faith than a ton of excitement. Trust in God alone…Never count upon immutability in man: inconstancy you may reckon upon without fear of disappointment."

Thirdly, continue to "serve God with all your might while the candle is burning, and then when it goes out for a season, you will have the less to regret."

Fourthly, "Be content to be nothing, for that is what you are. When your own emptiness is painfully forced upon your consciousness, chide yourself that you ever dreamed of being full, except in the Lord."

Lastly, "look for the recompensing joy hereafter. Continue, with double earnestness to serve the Lord when no visible result is before you." For Spurgeon, "Any simpleton can follow the narrow path in the light; faith's rare wisdom enables us to march on in the dark with infallible accuracy, since she places her hand in that of her Great Guide."

The lecture is concluded with the following exhortation: "Come fair or foul, the pulpit is our watchtower, and the ministry our warfare; be it ours, when we cannot see the face of God, to trust under the shadow of His wings."

A key component in preparing the preacher, without question, is learning how to avoid certain pitfalls unique to the ministry. The preacher must constantly examine himself. He must be true to himself, observing and evaluating the good and the bad pertaining to his character, life, and ministry. Such probing is not always comfortable for a preacher, but it is essential to the fulfillment of his ministry.

A gospel preacher must never forget that he is first and foremost a "man of God." "But flee from these things, you man of God, and pursue righteousness, godliness, faith, love, perseverance and gentleness" (1 Timothy 6:11). Every preacher must realize that sin is lurking at the door and its desire is to have dominion of him. The devil knows that if he can conquer the faith of the preacher, the flock may soon follow.

No preacher is God, although some may seem to deify him! Preachers are human and as such are subjected to the same temptations, trials, and pitfalls as are "common to man." The preacher must know that his need for daily renewal and repentance is no less real or necessary than any other in the kingdom. Paul had to bring his body into subjection to the will of God, lest after he preached to others, he would become castaway. Preachers must "go and do likewise" today.

In nineteenth-century America, a preacher named Benjamin Franklin (1812-1878) rose to great prominence in the church in for his fidelity to the word of God. His biographer relayed brother Franklin's words of wisdom for preachers in the following paragraphs. Consider these thoughts: "All we have to do to stand right before the people, is to be sound in heart, in the faith, in the life; true to the gospel of our Lord Jesus Christ; honest and faithful in the whole matter; maintaining, defending, advocating it as the only divine and gracious system for the salvation of a lost world;

enforcing it on men for its own sake, and for the sake of humanity."[11] Moreover, "May we all maintain soundness in the faith, in the gospel, integrity to it, faithfulness to it in all things, soundness in character, purity and holiness. May we strive to live nearer and still nearer to God."[12] Therefore, "It is not inventive genius we need in the church, nor explorers to invent something new, or to make new discoveries; but we need humble and honest men, who know and love the truth and will press it on the world."[13]

Leisure Time

Most preachers are not required to punch a time clock. Usually, it is assumed on good faith that the preacher will provide an honest day of work for an honest day of pay. What is self-responsibility for one can be a pitfall to another. A preacher must never forget that he is called to do "the work of an evangelist." Only by performing his work can he fulfill his ministry. The preacher must take the charge to "be not slothful" as personally and responsibly as anyone in the kingdom. He must strive to be a "doer of the word and not a *preacher* only."

The preacher's work ethic should never come into question if he is faithful to his calling. The use of his time will be wisely distributed among his many ministerial duties. However, there is a temptation for some preachers to become distracted in their liberty to use their time as they see fitting. Facebook has become a pitfall to the preacher and the profitable use of his time. Younger preachers are attracted to video games and would rather spend their afternoons leisurely playing them. Sports, golf, fishing, hunting, and the like can become distractions too.

---

[11] Otis Castleberry, *They Heard Him Gladly* (Rosemead, CA: Old Paths Publishing, 1963), 35.
[12] Ibid.
[13] Ibid, 39.

While it is true that the preacher should realize the importance of personal time for his physical and mental health, as well as the time he should give to his family, he must never forget about the time he is to give to the ministry of the word. If he believes he can give God only half-days here and there while expecting the church to support him with a fulltime salary, he is essentially attempting to rob God.

Equally wicked is his refusal to spend his time searching the scriptures. It is one thing to lose time for study because of being busy with calls, visits, and personal Bible studies; and it is an entirely different issue to choose not to study or work so that time can be spent in activities of lesser importance. The consequence of this refusal to study and work is self-righteousness. The preacher who does not study the word will only become wise in his own opinions. He will inevitably become self-righteous. Instead of being a workman, and handling accurately the word of God, he will take shortcuts in his studies. He will find himself defending the opinions of others without doing the necessary study to see if those things are true. He will parrot the dogmas of his favorite preacher instead of forming his conclusions from time well-spent with the word of God. Tradition will become truth to him without him ever truly realizing what has happened.

The laziness of a preacher will not only rob God, and the church, but it will rob the preacher of the necessary time needed to do his work, grow in his faith, and learn from the scriptures. He will lose the respect and influence he has among the church and the community. Moreover, he will give a bad reputation to other ministers who are attempting to labor until harvest has come.

The preacher must constantly examine himself. He must be true to himself, observing and evaluating the good and the bad pertaining to his character, life, and ministry. Such probing is not always comfortable for a preacher, but it is essential to the fulfillment of his ministry.

Concerning Criticism

Criticism, if handled improperly, can become a pitfall for ministers. It is safe to say that any man who has preached more than a time or two has been criticized by someone. Sometimes the criticisms are frivolous; yet, at other times, they are quite valid. A preacher should possess the wisdom to tell the difference. If we are to be perfectly honest, very few criticisms are immediately welcomed. Not every criticism is offered with the appropriate tone or at the appropriate time. Whether valid or not, criticisms should never cause a preacher to lose heart, or to give up his ambition to preach the gospel. But this is exactly what they can do.

Criticisms can pound away at a man until he begins to believe it. Unfair criticism can cause a preacher to feel utterly unworthy and unfit for ministry. Criticisms of the preacher's family can be especially hurtful and often unnecessary. A man may begin to wonder why he is sacrificing for people who do not love him. He may lose sight of God during this period of discouragement. The preacher may begin to feel as Paul did toward the church at Corinth when he lamented, "the more I love you the less I am loved." He may very well become "weary in well doing."

A man can prepare for criticism by remembering that man's rejection does not always indicate God's rejection. Our Lord had people reject Him too. At times, rejection may stem from the preaching of the truth and the rebuking of sin. At other times, criticism stems from a lack of wisdom on the part of the one doing the criticizing. In such cases, the preacher is innocent of wrongdoing and, as Stephen did, he must learn to pray "Lord, do not charge them with this sin."

Consider an example from another prominent preacher from nineteenth century America. His name was Tolbert Fanning (1810-1874). Brother Fanning was a great gospel preacher, educator, and editor of brotherhood papers from middle Tennessee. When he was a young man, just beginning to preach, an elderly sister told him, "You have made a failure. You are neither called nor qualified to preach. You ought not to try. You will disgrace the cause."[14] After inspecting his homemade suit of clothes and lanky frame, one brother told him, "Brother Fanning, you never can preach, and will always run your legs too far through your breeches. Do go home and go to plowing."[15]

Ignorance and spitefulness produce such criticisms. We might ask, who gave these people the right and the role to judge brother Fanning in that way? Where would churches of Christ in America be today had Tolbert Fanning gone home and gone to plowing? We would not have the paper he founded – the *Gospel Advocate*. We might not have been influenced by the men he trained to preach and influenced at Franklin College, the school he founded. These men include William and David Lipscomb, E.G. Sewell, E.A. Elam, T.B. Larimore, and J.W. Shepherd. Consider the combined sermons, articles, books, schools founded, classes taught, and souls converted and strengthened to live more faithful lives because of these men.

Moreover, Fanning and these men helped to stop the movement to use mechanical instruments of music in worship and the missionary society in evangelism among the congregations in the South. Thankfully, Tolbert Fanning did not allow these unfair criticisms to stop him from preaching! Had he "gone home and gone

---

[14] James Wilburn, *The Hazard of the Die* (Malibu, CA: Pepperdine University Press, 1980), 22-23.
[15] Ibid.

to plowing" he would have been guilty of putting his hand to God's plow, and looking back, he would have proven himself unfit for the kingdom of God (Luke 9:62).

Allow us to offer three rules of wisdom for preachers to apply when they are criticized. In the first place, consider the source of the criticism. Not all opinions are equal. For instance, if a preacher is being criticized by a murmuring, unhappy, unpleasant individual, who complains about everything and everyone, that should be noted. In such cases, the preacher is likely only the most recent brunt of this person's problems. In fact, many times this type of individual will voice their criticisms through "anonymous" letters. A preacher must never take to heart any criticism coming from a person who does not have the courage to sign their name. On the other hand, if the criticism is coming from a faithful and considerate person who truly has the best interest of the church and the preacher at heart, this too must be considered. It is likely that their advice will serve the preacher very well in his efforts to bring souls to Christ.

Secondly, compare the criticism with the scriptures. A person may be criticizing the preacher because of a sinful agenda or simply because they are ignorant about the Bible. Any criticism that would cause a preacher to compromise the truth should be avoided. Criticism becomes a great pitfall to a minister when he ceases to preach faithfully because of fearing or desiring to please the one doing the criticizing. However, if the criticism will help the preacher to provide a better understanding and application of the Bible through his preaching, then let him be thankful that he received such correction (cf. Proverbs 13:1; 15:10).

Thirdly, when faced with a malicious and miserable Christian, who relishes opportunities to criticize others, the preacher must not forget about the many good and dear souls who love him and have been brought closer to God through his preaching and labors.

The best people the preacher will ever know, and his closest friends, will be faithful members of the body of Christ. These dear souls must be considered before the criticism of the ungodly provokes him to quit.

If the criticism is valid and scriptural, then the preacher should make the necessary changes. "Fools despise wisdom and instruction." We should never be too proud to welcome helpful advice. A man should want to do his best at preaching because God deserves his best. Giving one's best will require honest self-examination and adjustment at times. Men devoted to preaching the gospel should allow valid criticisms to prepare them for greater service in their preaching and ministry.

Pride Goes before a Fall

Conversely to the criticisms preachers hear are the compliments he hears. One must be careful not to let compliments go to his head. Everyone loves a compliment. Some just love compliments more than others. There is a story about Alexander the Great. It is said that he had an advisor, who followed him around during parades and such, whose only job was to whisper in his ear, "You are Mortal. You are just a man. You are Mortal." As a man is preparing his life for ministry, perhaps he needs to hire such an assistant! Preachers are often told they are the "best" and that their sermon was the "greatest." *You are mortal. You are just a man.*

Just as a preacher must judiciously consider criticism, he must also carefully weigh the compliments he receives. He must be careful not to believe his own publicity, especially when it is good. After all, who among us can truthfully claim that he has already attained and is already perfected? No man should "think too highly" of himself. Every preacher has, and will always have, room for improvement. The point being: preachers must remain sober-minded – not too high or too low in their self-esteem. Neither success or failure in ministry should cause a preacher to stray from an abiding trust in God and His control over our lives.

Sadly, pride and the desire to have a "big name" and be the "best preacher" can cause preachers to compete rather than cooperate. Having notoriety does not make one sound in faith. Soundness is not found in trying to appear better than your fellow laborer in the kingdom. Men who have labored for self-advancement may advance themselves in their standing with those who are like-minded, but they will rarely advance the kingdom of God. The truly sound gospel preacher is confident in his life and doctrine and has no need to compete for the affection of the brotherhood.

Neither do they need to commend themselves. Bragging about oneself is an unfortunate practice that often comes out in some preaching. A prideful preacher will usually tell a lot about himself and a little about Christ. Stories of self-aggrandizement will never bring a person closer to Christ, break the stubborn will, or renew the spirit of the mind. Going to heaven is not dependent on knowing the preacher but knowing Christ. The story of Christ provides the power to reform, transform, and melt the hardest of hearts. Therein lies the power in preaching, ministry, and life.

Moreover, a preacher has no need to commend himself if he is commended by God. Hear Paul on the matter, "For we dare not class ourselves or compare ourselves with those who commend themselves. But they, measuring themselves by themselves, and comparing themselves among themselves, are not wise" (2 Corinthians 10:12).

The church of Christ in the city of Corinth had men who made no secrets of their personal animosity for Paul, claiming that he was not an apostle, and that he was strong in letter and weak in presence, implying that he would not be as bold face to face. Contrariwise, Paul never sought the recognition of his brethren. He was blessed to be able to help and thankful to those who appreciated his efforts; but he was never in competition with other faithful preachers. The devil was his competition. Paul knew that his works and teachings were enough to validate his ministry. He did not have to brag to receive any confirmation from his brethren. If his ministry was not confirmation enough, so be it.

Everyone likes to know they are appreciated by those they love. Even a dog likes to be told he is a good boy. But being told and being a great preacher are often two different cases. It does little good in eternity to be told how inspiring one is when in truth he has inspired very little. "Pride goes before a fall." Pride remains the "condemnation of the devil." A preacher must remain humble enough to improve in his service to God even when everyone around him tells him how great he is. Christ is the great one. His name is to be exalted. His name is above all names. Let every preacher remember, *"You are mortal. You are just a man. You are mortal."*

Here we have the essential characteristics of the gospel preacher expressly stated. He must be an honest man who knows and loves the truth and is ready to preach it. If he is not a man of such holy consecration, a man of God, his sins will eventually find him out. Some of the temptations placed before him may be willingly engaged; and some traps are truly pitfalls. A preacher might unwittingly stumble upon some evil lurking and be overcome. In preparing the man to preach, he must know about these things, however unpleasant they may be to discuss. He must learn to "walk circumspectly" and keep his soul with all diligence.

And to the Doctrine - 1 Timothy 4:16

The purpose of Paul's instruction to Timothy is to "save yourself and those who hear you" (1 Timothy 4:16). For this reason, the preacher is charged to "Take heed to yourself and unto the doctrine." The doctrine, or teachings, of the Christian pulpit can only be styled *Christian*, if the preaching is good, right, and true to the Word.

The primary work of the preacher, and church for that matter, is the preaching of the gospel. No work ever engaged by Christians has supplanted it. We may begin and continue benevolent and edifying ministries, bringing much good to our fellowman, but unless we are preaching the gospel, no one is being saved and man will remain in sin. The fundamental work of the ministry of Christ was to "bear witness of the truth" and "call sinners to repentance." As servants of His, we need not think our ministry is any different.

Our Lord did not come to establish a new political or economic system. He did not come to address every trivial quibble among men. Jesus came to address one concern – man in sin. His miracles, His teachings, His death, and His resurrection point to one issue – sin's consequences and cure.

The world is attempting to address the symptoms of sin but can never cure it. Only the gospel of Christ can cure sin. Our Lord would have us to deal with sin. If man's rebellion to God is changed, the world will change too.

Here is the problem with much modern preaching. Preachers are calling for men to reform and for the world to improve without the heart of the gospel being preached. It cannot be done. How can the world know love without God? How can the world have hope without Christ? How can humanity truly know inspiration without the Holy Spirit? How can man fathom absolute truth without the gospel?

At the heart of every great revival, and at the core of every great church, is steadfast, earnest, passionate, courageous, gospel preaching. "The mass of men are waiting for preaching of the New Testament kind, with a great message of grace to meet human need, delivered by men who realize that they represent a Throne, and have the right to claim submission to it."[1]

Men who have given themselves to the ministry of the word of Lord are essentially seeking to use their lives to help their fellow-man know the truth and be saved. True preaching is not merely the imparting of information for the sake of learning. True preaching is not calling upon men to be good moral and upright citizens, or patriots. True preaching insists upon an application being made by the hearer that might save his soul from death while reconciling him to his Father in heaven. The gospel is imparted by the preacher so that a person hearing can learn the truth of his condition and *obey* the blessed message before the sands of time empty from his earthen vessel. Only when the gospel is preached and obeyed is the hearer's relationship made right with God and the world will subsequently be changed for the better.

The only way to change the world from its wretchedness in sin and rebellion to God is to convert the world to Christ; and true conversion must occur. A man can become morally upright to some degree and yet never be converted to Christ. He might make his standing in the world a little better, but he will have very little impact on those around him. For his change of life to be effective to the point of also changing the lives of others, the man needs to

---

[1] G. Campbell Morgan, *Preaching* (Grand Rapids, MI: Baker, 1974), 14.

be changed for Christ's sake through obedience to the gospel. "How shall they hear without a preacher?"

Now we have the reason for preaching: "Let a man have the firm belief that he is dealing with immortal souls; that unless these souls embrace the Lord Jesus Christ and live in obedience to His laws, they must perish everlastingly; and that he is set to persuade them...being earnest in his appeals to them."[2]

What Is Preaching?

The problem with the world is sin. The world is as it is because men are living in sin. Untold social and economic efforts have been made to treat the symptoms, but only the gospel can provide the cure. Preaching is the application of the cure; the medicine is contained in the message. As man repents of his sin, the symptoms perpetuated by sin vanish from his life.

Biblical preaching is a proclamation of truth intended to appeal to the spiritual as well as the intellectual nature of man. It requires the whole of God's word being imparted to the whole of man, from the whole of man. Through biblical preaching, we address the intellect, awaken the spirit, and appeal to the will of the listener. We encourage those listening to be "doers of the word and not hearers only" (James 1:22).

Biblical preaching is not just a matter of style, taste, or preference. Whether or not one preaches the word of God is a matter of authority. That which distinguishes the message of the gospel preacher from the message of the world is the authority by which the message is spoken.

---

[2] William M. Taylor, *The Ministry of the Word* (Grand Rapids, MI: Baker, 1975), 135.

Many years ago, the venerable Cled E. Wallace wrote the following:

"Much is being said about the right kind of preaching and writing. Charges of 'hard' and 'soft' are being bandied back and forth. With as plain a book as the New Testament in hand, and with its abundant supply of examples of the very best preaching and writing, it ought not to be a difficult thing to determine the kind of both that should be done. A direct appeal to the New Testament, its preachers and its writers, ought to settle any question that arises in such a connection. Men who say the most about 'the right method of approach,' 'constructive articles,' etc., betray the fact that a lot of their ideas come from modern psychology, materialistic philosophy, and sectarian sources rather than from Jesus and the apostles. It is futile to do a lot of talking about the method of approach, when you never approach. It would improve some preachers and writers if they could forget about the method and go ahead and approach. The main idea is getting there anyhow."[3]

This article was written in June of 1939, and it is as timely as ever. In fact, more preachers than ever, it seems, rely upon "modern psychology, materialistic philosophy, and sectarian sources rather than from Jesus and the apostles" when it comes to their "preaching." They hide behind their false conception of Paul's charge to "speak the truth in love" while disregarding the divinely recorded sermons he preached. If one desires to know what Paul meant when he told us to speak the truth in love, go to the examples of his sermons and see how he did it.

In these words of encouragement to Timothy, Paul defines the subject of biblical preaching: "Preach the word! Be ready in sea-

---

[3] Cled E. Wallace, *Bible Banner*, Vol. 1, Num. 11, June 1939

son and out of season. Convince, rebuke, exhort, with all longsuffering and teaching" (2 Timothy 4:2). Biblical preaching demands preaching the word – whether it is popular or not. It requires preaching doctrine or "teaching" in a way that will "convince, rebuke, and exhort" the hearer. "The truth is, no preaching ever had any strong power that was not the preaching of doctrine."[4] Moreover, "every sermon must have a solid rest on Scripture, and the pointedness which comes of a clear subject, and the conviction which belongs to well-thought argument, and the warmth that proceeds from earnest appeal."[5] "The sermon is truth and man together; it is truth brought through man."[6]

The Purpose of the Sermon

Before any sermon is preached, the preacher must ask himself, "What is the purpose of my sermon?" In his book, *Saddlebags, City Streets, and Cyberspace (A History of Preaching in the Churches of Christ)*,[7] Michael W. Casey gave good attention to the impact of speech training among preachers in the second half of the twentieth century. Casey researched a drift that occurred from message/truth-oriented sermons to the audience/ listener-oriented preaching that is prevalent today. The primary difference in the two styles is that one is devoted to the content of the sermon primarily and the other seems to be more concerned with how the sermon is being received by the listener.

When focused solely on the reception of the sermon, preachers can be tempted to avoid any preaching might be deemed even

---

[4] Brooks, *Lectures on Preaching*, 129.
[5] Ibid., 131.
[6] Ibid., 158.
[7] Michael W. Casey, *Saddlebags, City Streets & Cyberspace* (Abilene, TX: ACU Press, 1995).

mildly controversial to placate the whims of the religious consumer. According to Haddon Robinson:

> "Those in the pulpit face the pressing temptation to deliver some message other than that of the Scriptures – a political system (either right-wing or left-wing), a theory of economics, a new religious philosophy, old religious slogans, or a trend in psychology...Yet when they fail to preach the scriptures, they abandon their authority. No longer do they confront their hearers with a word from God. That is why most modern preaching evokes little more than a wide yawn. God is not in it."[8]

The desire to please the audience prompted H.C. Brown, Jr., to write of the "clown prince of the pulpit." He observed, "the clown prince of the pulpit...is so addicted to the laughter and applause of the people that he constantly overuses it [humor]. Rather than sprinkling a little salt on steak, he sprinkles hamburger meat on blocks of salt."[9]

Over fifty years have passed since Brown's comment, and yet it is still commonplace to hear preachers giving lessons filled with personal testimonials and humorous anecdotes while offering very little of God and His divine truth. When preachers would rather be "the clown prince" than make known the "Prince of Peace," they devalue the work and the authority of the preacher in the contemporary world. When preachers forsake preaching the word of God, they forsake their authority and abandon their usefulness. Moreover, they portray a low view of scripture by refusing to preach it "in season and out of season."

---

[8] Haddon W. Robinson, *Biblical Preaching* (Grand Rapids, MI: Baker Academic, 2001), 20.

[9] H.C. Brown, Jr., *A Quest for Reformation in Preaching* (Nashville: Broadman Press, 1968), 18.

J.I. Packer spoke of the necessity for biblical preaching in that such preaching is of the "very essence" of Christianity.[10] Packer also observed that because of a lack of exegetical preaching among his fellowship, "there has been much non-preaching in our pulpits."[11] He stated that "preaching has come to be viewed as a human endeavor to please...[and] where interest centers upon spontaneity rather than substance, and passion in speakers is valued above preparation, true preaching must of necessity languish."

John R.W. Stott stated that some have rebelled against the preacher simply because he is an authority figure, and "Now everybody has his own opinions and his own convictions and considers them just as good as the preacher's."[12] When it comes to opinions, one opinion is as good as another. Which is even more reason for preachers to preach the word with "all authority" (Titus 2:15).

Preaching in the Modern Age

We live in a world that already has a low enough view of scripture, which is why preachers must remain even more vigilant in their deep reverence for the word of God. To reject the authority of the Bible is to reject the authority of God. Moreover, to judge the meaning of a scripture by anything other than God's intended purpose is to judge oneself unworthy to receive it. Jimmy Jividen observed, "some [brethren] have a low view of the Scriptures by regarding them as writing which must be interpreted experientially, culturally and relatively."[13]

---

[10] Samuel, T. Logan, Jr. (editor), *The Preacher and Preaching* (Phillipsburg, NJ: Presbyterian and Reformed Publishing Company, 1986), 2.

[11] Ibid, 3-5.

[12] John R.W. Stott, *Between Two Worlds* (Grand Rapids, MI: Eerdmans Publishing Company, 1982), 52.

[13] Jimmy Jividen, *More than a Feeling* (Nashville: Gospel Advocate Company, 1999), 138.

The experiential approach causes men to believe the Scripture says what "you feel it says" because you are interpreting its meaning based upon your own life experiences. The cultural approach has the meaning of the text changing with the times. And the relative approach is taken simply so that "you can have 'your truth' and I can have 'my truth.'"[14]

Our modern society has become weakened to the point of death through moral relativism. Christian values have been replaced with the notion of "all truth is truth." The teaching of Christian values, in many cases, requires beginning at square one. For this very reason Charles Colson addressed the need of "pre-evangelism" in cases where a person does not believe in God or morality.[15] The naturalist (atheistic) view has no treatment for sin. "Only the Christian concept of sin and moral responsibility gives us a rational way to understand and order our lives"[16] Modern society is acting irrationally today because they do not know Christ, and thus, do not understand sin, its consequences, and its cure. Today's scientists and philosophers have attempted to replace biblical morals and Christian virtues with a worldview that has no morals, no love, and no hope for life.

In order to preach the word in this century, preachers are going to have to become apologists in the field of Christian Evidences. Preachers are going to have to know and "be ready to give an answer" (1 Peter 3:15) in rebuttal to the atheistic false science being advocated today. We are going to have to educate a lost and dying world on the basic themes of God, sin, and man's redemption.

The present evil age needs the gospel and preachers with the backbone to preach it. Only in the gospel can one find God's

---

[14] Ibid., 139.
[15] Charles Colson and Nancy Pearcey, *How Now Shall We Live?* (Carol Stream, IL: Tyndale House Publishers, 1999), 30.
[16] Ibid., 198

power and authority to save. Biblical preaching is what is needed most. By preaching the gospel, preachers approach the intellect of the listeners with the intention to bring their respective wills into subjection to the will of God. Only through the gospel of the Son of God can "captivity be led captive" and true peace come to exist between God and man.

As a man of God, the preacher must believe in the power of God's word and determine to preach it. Avoid the pitfall of popularity propagated by pride. Honor is due the man who with humble faith and genuine piety stands for God, in the presence of God, to speak the word of God, to the people of God.

Truth in Love

Gus Nichols preached for many years in Jasper, Alabama. He died on November 16, 1975. Years before, and upon deciding to dedicate his life to preaching the gospel, his dear wife Matilda said to him, "If you are going to make a preacher, make a good one." She also gave this advice to her sons who dedicated their lives to preaching the gospel. Sister Nichols' words serve as great advice for preachers today. If you are determined to be a gospel preacher, determine to "make a good one." Be a gospel preacher.

Gospel preaching is speaking the truth in love. No matter what else is done, or how it is done, the truth must be spoken in love. Love must be the motivating factor for all that we do or say. Love, however, can require preaching some difficult lessons. Such provides a tense conundrum for the preacher. How can we (as preachers) meet the challenge of preaching hard sermons in love?

First let us dispel the notion that "hard preaching" is the antithesis to speaking the truth in love. If this is truly the case, Jesus would be guilty, for He taught hard sayings (John 6:60). People quit following the Lord because of His hard preaching (v. 66). God

Himself loves those whom He rebukes and chastens (Hebrews 12:5-6). God is love (1 John 4:16) and God rebukes and chastens.

Some people can be saved with compassion. Other people must be saved with fear (Jude 22). Paul said, "...knowing therefore the terror of the Lord, we persuade men" (2 Corinthians 5:11). Paul persuaded men by the terror of the Lord because he loved their souls. He was speaking the truth in love. Thus, a "negative sermon" may indeed be preached in truth and love.

Let us now dispel another false notion as some preachers seem overjoyed at the prospect of preaching a hard sermon. For them, it is an opportunity to prove to the audience that they are "sound," or to make a name for being sound. Such preachers equate sympathy and sensitivity with being "unsound." Of course, this would render Jeremiah as being unsound (Lamentations 3:48). It seems that both the one who refuses to preach a hard lesson for fear of loss, and the other who seizes the opportunity with the hope of gain, are preaching for selfish ambition (Philippians 1:16). In either case, love would not appear to be their motivation, but personal gain.

Truth with Boldness

In the same epistle which Paul encouraged us to speak the truth in love, he requested that the brethren in Ephesus would pray for him that he might "speak boldly, as I ought to speak" (Ephesians 6:20). True courage is essential to true preaching. "The wicked flee when no man pursues: but the righteous are bold as a lion" (Proverbs 28:1). Biblical examples of this proverb include:

- Jesus spoke boldly when exposing the error of the Pharisees (John 7:26).
- Peter and John spoke boldly in defending the truth against the accusations of the high counsel (Acts 4:13).

- Paul preached boldly at Damascus in the face of enemies who would attempt to take his life (Acts 9:27, 29).

- Paul and Barnabas spoke boldly in Iconium, while being resisted by disbelieving Jews (Acts 14:3).

- Apollos spoke boldly in the synagogue of Ephesus (Acts 18:26).

- Paul boldly preached in the same synagogue for three months – "disputing and persuading the things concerning the kingdom of God" (Acts 19:8).

- Paul and Barnabas waxed bold in the face of envious, con-tradicting Jews while preaching at Antioch of Pisidia (Acts 13:46).

- Paul was not afraid to write or speak boldly to his brethren at Rome (Romans 15:15), Corinth (2 Corinthians 7:4, 10:1-2, 11:21), and Thessalonica (1 Thessalonians 2:2) – or even unto Philemon (Philemon 8).

Every preacher should be so bold – "For God has not given us the spirit of fear; but of power, and of love, and of a sound mind" (2 Timothy 1:7). Every Christian should be able to say boldly, "The Lord is my helper, and I will not fear what man shall do unto me" (Hebrews 13:6). We are missing this element of boldness in our preaching which is fundamental to saving a lost and dying world. As with Joshua in the days of old, we too must "Be strong and of a good courage; be not afraid, neither be dismayed: for the LORD your God is with you wherever you go" (Joshua 1:9). The Lord has made the same promise to us as we fulfill His mission in this world (see Matthew 28:20).

But how we might become more courageous and speak with greater boldness? Begin by praying for boldness. The church in Jerusalem prayed that they could speak with boldness (Acts 4:29) and they did (v. 31). Paul asked for prayers that he could boldly teach and preach the word of God (Ephesians 6:19-20, Philippians 1:20), which he did. We too must offer this prayer for our sake and for the sake of our brethren. Study, Study, STUDY! As we learn the truth and know the truth (John 8:32), we will be more confident to teach the truth. Paul was not ashamed of the gospel because he knew what it was, and that he was in fact preaching the truth (Romans 1:16ff.).

Place fear in its proper place. Too many times we do nothing because we are afraid of making a mistake. Yet, the only One we need to fear is God (Matthew 10:26-28). "But and if you suffer for righteousness' sake, happy are you: and be not afraid of their terror, neither be troubled" (1 Peter 3:14). Rather than being troubled by what people might do or say, Peter teaches, "But sanctify the Lord God in your hearts: and be ready always to give an answer to every man that asks you a reason of the hope that is in you with meekness and fear" (v. 15). Ezekiel was due to face his critics. And the Lord told him not to be afraid of their words or dismayed at their looks (2:6), but to listen to Him and speak His word (v. 7). The Lord told Jeremiah the same concerning the hardened faces of the people the prophet would address.

"Therefore prepare yourself and arise, And speak to them all that I command you. Do not be dismayed before their faces, Lest I dismay you before them. For behold, I have made you this day a fortified city and an iron pillar, And bronze walls against the whole land—Against the kings of Judah, Against its princes, Against its priests, And against the people of the land. They will fight against you, But they shall not prevail against you. For I am with you," says the Lord, "to deliver you" (Jeremiah 1:17-19).

Remember that we will face the Lord in judgment and give an answer for what we did and did not do (James 4:17). Paul could truthfully say that he was free from the blood of all men because he had the boldness to preach the whole counsel of God (Acts 20:26-27). Can we say the same?

Refrain from criticizing your brethren who have the courage to speak boldly. Oftentimes, we are our worst enemy in this regard. Do you find it interesting how some of our brethren are willing to rebuke the one who has boldness and cares enough to correct the erring brother, but will not rebuke the soul bringing shame and reproach upon the church? They are bold enough to criticize the person who is attempting to do the right thing, but cowardly shrink away from doing the right thing themselves. When we act this way, we strain out the gnat and swallow the camel (Matthew 23:24). Moreover, when we act this way, we discourage our brethren who have boldness, rather than encourage them to use their boldness as a blessing.

We must dispel the notion that boldness is ugliness. Certainly, our Lord was not being ugly when He was speaking boldly. Boldness is not ugliness. Boldness is having the courage to teach the truth even when it is not welcomed. The best way to dispel this notion is for our brethren who are so bold to be careful to season their speech with grace when necessary (Colossians 4:6). Give your critics nothing to criticize. Yet, if they persist in their criticisms, "Be strong and of a good courage" (Joshua 1:6), for you are doing the right thing.

Draw strength from others who are bold in the truth. Paul's example, even despite suffering, helped others to speak the word with boldness (Philippians 1:14). We can do the same by setting the right example. None of us should want to go to the final judgment with blood on our hands because we were too afraid to speak the truth. By caring enough to teach the lost we will offer a sweet savor to the Lord, regardless of the results (2 Corinthians 2:14-

17). Let us have the courage to obey the Lord, and the boldness to speak the truth in love.

Preaching Style

A man's style of preaching is about as important to the overall result of his efforts as is a person's style of handwriting. If the handwriting is legible (understandable), and the spelling is correct, the style simply becomes a bonus. So it is with preaching: if the sermon is correct and full of truth, and understandable, much good can come regardless of style. It seems many are paying more attention to the preacher's style than they are to the content, understandability, and correctness of his message. The comparison of styles has done much to promote competition among preachers as well.

The sum of all we might contribute to this subject can be said in relatively few words. Let the preacher first be thoroughly biblical in his message. "Preach the word." "Speak as the oracles of God." "Serve God rather than man." Nothing beyond this point of emphasis matters, if the message is not founded upon the bedrock of God's divinely inspired word.

With a clear aim to preach the truth on the subject or text in mind, let him be earnest and sincere. As he drinks of the sincere milk of the word, may it become part of him and flow through him through words of sincere, tender, and earnest pleadings. Let him be courageous, standing in the shadow of the cross, quickening the hearts and stirring the conscious of his audience to submit to the divine truth he is presenting. Let his language be clear and precise, avoiding the theological terminology besetting our field of study, language which is only known to professors and seminarians. Speak so plainly that a child can understand. If the baby calf can reach the straw, the mama and daddy can too.

The preacher must be true to himself and speak with the "ability God gives." A minister who is free, honest, true, and sincere with himself and with the word he handles will be much more likely to find these qualities in those who receive his message. If he is fake and disingenuous, he will be perceived as a fraud, even though his message may be true. Let him avoid at all costs the temptation to imitate others. Can you imagine Hardeman imitating Keeble or vice versa? Both men were extremely effective in their preaching as they preached according to their own natural giftedness. But what was one man's success would have been the other man's failure. What is a man if he is not himself? "To thine own self be true!"

The pernicious practice of performing rather than preaching is all too commonplace in the modern pulpit. Feigning enthusiasm, strutting about like a banty rooster, hoping to appear hip and cool; demonstrative gestures, and the like, let them forever be anathema to the man who steps upon the rostrum to speak before the people of God. If the congregation is there to witness a performance and be entertained by the preacher, then these souls are most in need of true gospel preaching. They must be taught out of their error if they are to grow in the grace and knowledge of the Lord.

As a matter of convenience, many preachers are using electronics in their presentation. But often these electronics are a distraction and detriment to his natural style. Any aid is good when used properly. Let the man of God be careful not to allow his electronics to become a detriment to his preaching. Use them sparingly. Keep your natural, free-flowing thoughts. Proclaim the word, instead of reading the screen. It will be impossible to "convert the sinner from the error of his way" if the preacher has read him to sleep in his sermon.

Let the preacher be free, be himself, be genuine, sincere, and earnest. May he with tender precision apply the gospel to the heart of the listener. May the soul wounded by sin find healing in the cross. A blessing will come from God to the man who in truth and love with great courage and boldness speaks to the world "the unsearchable riches of Christ."

Types of Sermons

Three types of sermons are commonly used – expository, textual, and topical. These three categories can be subdivided *ad nauseum,* but we shall limit our discussion to a very general description overall.

Expository

An expository sermon takes its topic, points, and subpoints from a single passage of scripture. Some of the richest and most meaningful expository preaching to be done is from the Bible's narratives. For example, a preacher may want to address the issue of division among brethren by preaching from the story of Abraham and Lot (Genesis 13). The preacher may want to teach how a person is converted to Christ by preaching from the narrative of Saul's conversion (Acts 9, 22, 26). It could be that church leadership needs to be addressed and the preacher could choose to do so the selection of men to help minister to widows in Acts 6. Whatever need may arise you can generally depend upon a narrative to address it. Preaching the narrative in an expository way allows the immediate text of the narrative to be studied exclusively and thoroughly.

Character studies can also be done through expository preaching. Events in the life of Elijah, Paul, or Christ could take shape through an expository presentation.[17]

---

[17] The sermons of William M. Taylor serve as an excellent example of this type of preaching.

How does a preacher select the appropriate narrative from scripture or event in the life of a Bible character to meet a need?

- ➢ Look for similarities in circumstances and personalities.

- ➢ Look for statements which can clearly point to the matter you are addressing. For example, "Let there be no strife…for we are brethren" (Genesis 13:8).

- ➢ Look for narratives that can be plainly understood and where an acceptable application of God's word was made. For example, the Ethiopian Eunuch (Acts 8) provides us with an example of someone who was studying, a preacher who taught him about the Lord, the decision to be baptized, and the joy that followed.

- ➢ Look for narratives where God's word is rejected and the resulting punishment for disobedience. Why was God's word disobeyed? What could have been done differently? How might the circumstances have changed for the better if God's word had been obeyed? An example of such a narrative would be David and Bathsheba (2 Samuel 11-12).

Expository preaching is also done by taking texts from scripture that are not necessarily narrative or character studies, analyzing them in their context, and then presenting the message of the text in an understandable way to the listeners. The following principles have been adapted from Michael Gorman, *Elements of Biblical Exegesis.*[18]

- ➢ Provide a Survey of the Text – preparation and overview, introduction.

---

[18] Michael J. Gorman, *Elements of Biblical Exegesis* (Grand Rapids, MI: Baker, 2009), 63ff.

- ➢ Analyze the Context of the Text – historical and literary.

- ➢ Analyze the Form, Structure, and Movement of the Text – people, setting, dialogue.

- ➢ What is the "Big Picture" of the Text? What are the Main Points of the Text?

- ➢ Reflection – text for today; application for today.

- ➢ Expansion and Refinement – review and refine what you have learned before preaching.

Textual

Textual preaching can refer to a couple of different methods, depending on the book you are reading. For preachers of the nineteenth century, textual preaching was equated with the preaching of Charles Spurgeon. He would take one verse or small passage of scripture for his topic and main points. Then he would supplement the main points with statements found elsewhere in scripture. Martyn Lloyd Jones also used this method effectively in the twentieth century. For preachers of today, this type of preaching is akin to Bible class teaching as a preacher will work through a text verse-by-verse supplementing his thoughts with other passages of scripture.

An example of textual preaching would be to take the text of John 3:16 and divide according to the thoughts gleaned from the statement – e.g., the existence of God, the love of God, the grace of God, the Son of God, the gospel of God. As each new point is introduced, passages or statements from elsewhere in scripture are given in support of the main point. The preacher is not relying solely on John 3:16, or the immediate context, but also on similar passages of scripture throughout the Bible.

Topical

Topical preaching involves a collection of scriptures connected by a particular theme or subject. The church will always have a need for topical preaching. If you decide to preach about the music of the church, you will likely need to preach a topical sermon. Many issues will arise, and many questions will be asked that must be answered in a topical way. Topical preaching does not require that the expository method be abandoned. You may want to preach about baptism. To do so, you will have to exegete the relevant passages, collect your findings, and then present them accordingly. You would have preached a topical sermon on baptism while still providing an exposition of the relevant texts. One helpful tip for writing topical sermons is to ask the questions who, what, when, where, and why.

Many of the classic sermon books by preachers from the churches of Christ contain examples of topical sermons. J.W. McGarvey's sermons on inspiration and repentance are excellent examples of the topical method.

Sermon Development

Dennis M. Cahill provides four phases of sermon development. The following has been adapted from Dennis M. Cahill, *The Shape of Preaching*.[19]

1.) **From Text to Sermon Focus** – having identified the text you intend to preach, what is the main idea(s) of that passage? Cahill notes the exegetical idea (the meaning of the passage) and the homiletical idea (the application of the passage).

---

[19] Dennis M. Cahill, *The Shape of Preaching* (Grand Rapids, MI: Baker, 2007), 91ff.

2.) **From Focus to Sermon Form** – Different texts call for different types of sermons. What is the type of outline you intend to use in preaching the text or topic?

3.) **Developing the Sermon Form** – At this phase illustrations and explanations are added to enrich the sermon. What process is involved in developing and finishing the sermon?

- Initial notes
- The main idea
- Word studies
- Background material (History, geography, biography, etc.)
- Rough outline
- Introduction
- Finishing the outline (easy transitions from point to point)
- Enhancing the sermon (the use of illustrations, statistics, etc.)

4.) **Delivering the Sermon** – This is the final phase and involves the actual techniques involved in preaching the sermon. Such techniques include tone of voice, appearance, visual aids, etc.

Sermon Illustrations

Illustrations should serve to illuminate a point in the sermon. They must never take the place of the point or overshadow the message of the sermon itself. When used effectively, illustrations will help the hearer to remember and apply the point that has been made. Effective illustrations come from a wide variety of learning. The better the variety of interests the preacher has, the better his illustrations will be.

Types of Illustrations

1.) Biblical (characters, cross references from scripture, narratives)

2.) Historical (persons, events)

3.) Societal (present day issues, personalities)

4.) Ecclesiastical (church history)

5.) Personal (testimonial, personal experiences)

6.) Natural (plants, animals, space, time)

7.) Factual (statistics and data)

8.) Comical (humor)

9.) Scientific (laws of science, math)

10.)Geographical (places, scenery)

11.)Poetical (poetry, songs, stanzas, lyrics)

12.)Figures of Speech (allegory, metaphor, etc.)

13.)Quotations (well-known persons and applicable quotes)

14.)Practical (everyday occurrences and daily tasks)

15.)Philosophical (philosophies of men from history)

Hermeneutics and Homiletics

Hermeneutics is the science of interpreting meaning in literature. The term "sacred hermeneutics" refers to methods used for interpreting the Bible. The goal of hermeneutics is "exegesis." Exegesis occurs when the true meaning is "drawn out" of the text. A preacher will never be able to preach the truth on a text or subject without first interpreting the text or subject truthfully. Before we can preach the truth, we must know the truth. Whether we do so intentionally or unintentionally, if we have interpreted something incorrectly, we will be guilty of preaching error.

A traditional hermeneutic is centered upon the understanding that the Bible contains objective truth, commandments to be obeyed, and an original meaning which can be understood. The heart of the hermeneutic is to understand the meaning of God's word for mankind. Truth can be known, understood objectively, followed, obeyed, and taught. Adherents to the traditional hermeneutic might disagree about the meaning of the text, but they agree that the text does reveal a meaning to be understood.

A traditional homiletic is centered upon preaching God's word so that men might obey. Once the meaning of the text has been understood, it is the work of the preacher to communicate this meaning to his hearers. The communication of the text usually includes a series of propositions which have been ascertained by the preacher and are to be applied by the hearer.

Over the last half-century, a new hermeneutic has evolved. At the core of this new hermeneutic is the notion that the text means different things to different people. The text is to be encountered and each person is to decide what God is saying to him/her personally. The text says what a person hears it to say.

The new homiletic follows the new hermeneutic accordingly. The point of the sermon is not necessarily the distributing of information, but the stimulation of a feeling or emotion. The passage is to be preached as a story, narrative, or inductively. No conclusion or word of ultimate meaning or application is to be pressed by the preacher. The hearer is left free to make his/her personal application as the voice of the text speaks through the sermon. Stories, illustrations, etc., become the points of the sermon rather than a set of propositions.

The issue at hand is fundamental to one's approach to scripture and a preacher's proclamation of it. Exegesis is to draw out of the text its meaning. This is what we are to do in "handling accurately the word of truth." Eisegesis occurs when one reads his theology or theological presuppositions into the text, as did the scribes and Pharisees.

Theology should be derived from one's study of the scriptures rather than used to manipulate one's study of the scriptures. It is the responsibility of the preacher to understand the message of the Bible (theology) by utilizing sound methods of interpretation (hermeneutics) and then preaching that message to the listener with conviction (homiletics). One must be a good student of the scriptures before he can ever become a good expositor of the scriptures. Before power can be demonstrated in the pulpit, there must be diligent preparation in the study. The preacher must be informed of its meaning before he can inform others. He must be transformed by its truth before his sermon can effectively assist in transforming the lives of others.

Essentially, the new homiletic has become a poor preacher's attempt to evade the hard questions of the Bible and dodge any culpability of saying something which might be construed as negative or controversial. The responsibility to speak the "whole counsel of God" is ditched under the guise of letting the hearer decide for himself, as though that has not been happening all along through sermons based upon deductive reasoning.

The force and the power of the message preached is derailed as a locomotive that has jumped the tracks; and in its place are shenanigans of the most childish sort. The manliness of the pulpit is replaced with the gimmickry of "acting" and performing. As such, a preacher may dress in full costume to mimic a Bible character and act in the first person throughout his performance as though he was an actor in a play dramatizing the biblical text rather than proclaiming it.

Is this what we have come to? Are we so hardened and desirous of smooth speeches that we would make a kid out of our preacher; that we would turn him into our court jester; that we would make a fool out of him so that we might feel more entertained during this portion of the worship service? Who among us could imagine any of the legendary preachers of Restoration Movement donning a fake beard, bed sheet, and wig and claim to be John the Baptist?

While such foolishness persists, we ponder among ourselves why the church in America is in decline. Is it any wonder? God chose the preaching of the text as the means to save those who would believe (1 Corinthians 1:21), not acting, performing, or dramatizing the text. Such a pulpit is built on sand and destined to fall and great will be the fall of it.

Great Churches Have Great Preaching

The church in Thessalonica was a great church. Listen to the words used to describe them by Paul:

"We give thanks to God always for you all, making mention of you in our prayers, remembering without ceasing your **work of faith, labor of love, and patience of hope** in our Lord Jesus Christ in the sight of our God and Father, knowing, beloved brethren, your election by God. For our gospel did not come to you in word only, but also in power, and in the Holy Spirit and in **much assurance**, as you know **what kind of men we were** among you for your sake. And you became **followers** of us and of the Lord, having **received the word in much affliction**, with **joy of the Holy Spirit**, so that you **became examples** to all in Macedonia and Achaia who believe. For **from you the word of the Lord has sounded forth**, not only in Macedonia and Achaia, but also in every place. **Your faith toward God** has gone out, so that we do not need to say anything. For they themselves declare concerning us what manner of entry we had to you, and how **you turned to God from idols to serve the living and true God**, and **to wait for His Son** from heaven, whom He raised from the dead, even Jesus who delivers us from the wrath to come" (1 Thessalonians 1:2-10).

The great church at Thessalonica had faith, love, and hope which was manifest in their work, labor, and patience (endurance). This was a working church. They were an enduring church, having received (welcomed) the word of God in a time of "much affliction." The church was filled with wisdom and discernment, knowing, and being assured of the veracity of the gospel and the validity of the men who preached the word of grace to them.

Moreover, they were truly converted. Turning from idols to serve the living God and to wait for the Lord of glory to return, they became followers of Paul and the Lord in word and deed, sounding forth the message true and glad in Macedonia and Achaia. This was an evangelistic church! In so doing, they became examples of faith and faithfulness to others. They were humble, receptive, and proactive in the ministry of the word.

How did they become so stalwart in their convictions? It began with great preaching. At the heart of every great church is great preaching. Notice what is said in 1 Thessalonians 2:1-12:

"For you yourselves know, brethren, that our coming to you was not in vain. But even after we had suffered before and were spitefully treated at Philippi, as you know, **we were bold in our God to speak to you the gospel of God in much conflict**. For our exhortation did **not come from error or uncleanness, nor was it in deceit**. But as we have been approved by God to be entrusted with the gospel, **even so we speak, not as pleasing men, but God** who tests our hearts. For **neither at any time did we use flattering words**, as you know, nor a cloak for covetousness—God is witness. **Nor did we seek glory from men**, either from you or from others, when we might have made demands as apostles of Christ. But **we were gentle among you, just as a nursing mother cherishes her own children**. So, affectionately longing for you, we were well pleased **to impart to you not only the gospel of God, but also**

our own lives, because you had become dear to us. For you remember, brethren, **our labor and toil**; for laboring **night and day**, that we might not be a burden to any of you, **we preached to you the gospel of God**. You are witnesses, and God also, how **devoutly and justly and blamelessly we behaved** ourselves among you who believe; as you know how **we exhorted**, and **comforted**, and **charged** every one of you, **as a father does his own children**, that you would walk worthy of God who calls you into His own kingdom and glory" (1 Thessalonians 2:1-12).

During the Second Missionary Journey, Paul and his companions visited Thessalonica for the first time after being spitefully treated in Philippi. Even though their message was not welcomed by all in that city, they continued in doctrine, preaching the same gospel with boldness in the city of Thessalonica. These men preached the truth boldly, not with error, uncleanness, deceit, or flattering words. They were single-minded in their devotion to please and serve God rather than men. They came to Thessalonica humbly, not seeking glory from men, but that Christ may be glorified as the crucified Savior of the world.

Moreover, they came willing to work and to labor and toil night and day for the furtherance of the gospel and to support themselves. These men labored sacrificially, not superficially, willing to impart not only the word of truth, but their own lives if necessary. Their manner of life was devout, just, and blameless. They set the example of Christian virtue for the flock to follow.

Paul and his company also came with a spirit of tender compassion, as a nursing mother cherishes her children, and as a godly father exhorts, comforts, and charges his children. With men of God like these in their midst, and the truth of the gospel being exemplified and imparted through them, is it any wonder that the church in Thessalonica became such a fine congregation? Paul and these men were bold in their proclamation of truth, they understood their responsibility as ministers in behavior and work, they sought to please God first and foremost, they were gentle and affectionate to the people, and they were sacrificial with their money, love, and time.

If we can imitate the example of these men as ministers of the gospel today, our congregations will also be more likely to mirror the church we read about in Thessalonica.

Paul's Ministry in Ephesus

Paul's ministry in Thessalonica was not an anomaly. He practiced and preached the same doctrine – *continuing in them* – everywhere he went. He spent three years in Ephesus, perhaps the longest he stayed in any one city. In Acts 20:17ff., we have Paul's description of his ministry in Ephesus. He is concluding his Third Missionary Journey and meeting with the elders of the church as they traveled from Ephesus to Miletus.

"From Miletus he sent to Ephesus and called for the elders of the church. And when they had come to him, he said to them: 'You know, from the first day that I came to Asia, in what manner I always lived among you, **serving the Lord with all humility**, with **many tears and trials** which happened to me by the plotting of the Jews; how **I kept back nothing that was helpful**, but **proclaimed** it to you, and **taught** you **publicly** and **from house to house, testifying to Jews, and also to Greeks**, **repentance** toward God and **faith** toward our Lord Jesus Christ...And indeed, now I know that you all, among whom **I have gone preaching the kingdom of God**, will see my face no more. Therefore I testify to you this day that I am innocent of the blood of all men. For I have **not shunned to declare to you the whole counsel of God**... Therefore watch, and remember that for three years **I did not cease to warn everyone night and day with tears**...I have **coveted no one's silver or gold or apparel**. Yes, you yourselves know that **these hands have provided for my necessities**, and for those who were with me. **I have shown you in every way, by laboring like this, that you must support the weak**...And when he had said these things, he knelt down and **prayed**..."

While Paul was in Ephesus, he carried himself as a humble servant of the Lord, "serving the Lord with all humility." Even though he shed many tears and suffered trials, he kept nothing back that was helpful, and taught the whole counsel of God. Alluding to Ezekiel's charge from God (Ezekiel 3:19ff.), Paul could say that he too was free from the blood of all men. If the citizens of Ephesus chose not to repent and obey the gospel, it would not be because Paul failed to teach them.

Paul boldly proclaimed the gospel (cf. Acts 19:8) and taught personally from house to house. He testified – both bearing witness and protesting solemnly – to the Jews and Greeks alike of turning to God and believing in Christ, showing no discrimination. He warned night and day with tears, preaching the kingdom of God.

No man could say Paul coveted their belongings, or that he was a freeloader. He earned his keep by laboring with his own hands, even teaching them to support the weak through their livelihood.

When we read Paul's epistle to the Ephesians, we find more evidence of the great love and admiration Paul had for the church. No document in the New Testament is more focused on the nature of the church as the spiritual body of Christ than Paul's epistle to the Ephesians. Love was the motivation for Paul's ministry, his preaching, and his exemplary life.

If ministers of the word can learn to love the church as Paul did, and appreciate the value of healthy churches to God and to man, how much more earnest will be our efforts to build up the body of Christ? Would our labors increase? Would devotion of this sort stir more sacrificial love? Would foolish pride diminish and glory to God be exalted? Think of the good that could come if we will only remember and focus on the purpose and responsibility of our work as heralds of the gospel of Christ, the hope within us, and the grace that sets men free.

Maxims of the Restoration Plea

Preachers in America have been blessed to live in a country which grants its citizens the right to religious freedom. We have a religious freedom that is unprecedented in this world's history. More than two hundred years ago devout Bible students, preachers, and church leaders used this freedom to return to the teachings of the Bible and restore the church of the New Testament in this country.

Many will find in family history parents, grandparents, and great-grandparents who came out of the darkness of religious error and returned to a religion based solely on the word of God. In their approach to the scriptures, these pious souls used certain fundamental principles to guide them. These maxims are just as essential today as ever before. They are right, not because of who said them, or even who believed them, but because they are derived from the word of God. When considering the message the church is receiving from their preachers, we must consider these fundamental truths.

"Where the scriptures speak, we speak; and where the scriptures are silent, we are silent." Man has always been instructed and restricted not to go beyond the boundaries of divine revelation. At the giving of the Law of Moses we read: "You shall not

add to the word which I command you, neither shall you diminish from it, that you may keep the commandments of the LORD your God which I command you" (Deuteronomy 4:2). At the conclusion of the Book of Revelation we read a similar warning not to "add unto these things" or to "take away from the words of the book of this prophecy" (Revelation 22:18-19).

The scriptures not only teach the principle, but also give examples of how to obey it. Paul and Apollos set an example before the church that they "might learn in us not to think of men above that which is written" (1 Corinthians 4:6). Furthermore, "those who are measuring themselves by themselves, and comparing themselves among themselves, are not wise" (2 Corinthians 10:12).

The authority of the message preached is limited by the word of God. When man goes beyond the word, he steps beyond the authority vested in him by God. Usually, the man begins to meddle and major in minors. Not uncommon, however, is the sinister result of dividing the church and causing more sectarianism in a world already rife with it.

"No Creed but the Bible." "Raccoon" John Smith and John Rogers joined with Barton W. Stone and John T. Johnson in a series of unity discussions. The four men decided to call a general meeting to discuss the unity of their groups at Georgetown, Kentucky on December 23-26, 1831.

A second meeting was conducted over the New Year's weekend in Lexington, Kentucky. Smith was the spokesman for the Campbell group, and after having pled for unity, concluded by saying: "Let us, then, my brethren, be no longer Campbellites or Stoneites, New Lights or Old Lights, or any other kind of lights, but let us come to the Bible and to the Bible alone, as the only book in the world that can give us all the light we need." On this basis he and Stone extended the right hand of fellowship to each other to symbolize the unity of the two groups.

You will observe that this too is a biblical principle. After all, who is to say which doctrines should be included in a creed and which doctrines should be excluded? If a creed is one doctrine shy of the New Testament, it is too small for Christians. If it has one doctrine too many, it is too large for Christians. The purpose for creeds in the Protestant world is to distinguish one denominational church from another. However, all that has ever been needed to distinguish the Lord's church from the world – the saved from the lost – is the testimony of the word of God (John 8:47).

The word of God must be our standard – nothing more, nothing less (John 12:48). If we will follow the Bible, and the Bible alone, we will walk by the same rule and mind the same thing (Philippians 3:16). Doctrines and opinions of men have always and will always divide Christians. If we will do away with them, and walk by faith in the word of God, we will come nearer to restoring the unity of all believers.

"In matters of faith – unity; in matters of opinion – liberty; in all things – charity." Restoration leaders followed the Lord and His apostles by urging unity in matters of faith. Paul wrote, "Now I plead with you, brethren, by the name of our Lord Jesus Christ, that you all speak the same thing, and that there be no divisions among you, but that you be perfectly joined together in the same mind and in the same judgment" (1 Corinthians 1:10).

The great apostle also urged liberty in matters of opinion. He wrote, "Finally, brethren, farewell. Become complete. Be of good comfort, be of one mind, live in peace; and the God of love and peace will be with you" (2 Corinthians 13:11).

Of course, he also stated that love was the greatest of all. "Love suffers long and is kind; love does not envy; love does not parade itself, is not puffed up; does not behave rudely, does not seek its own, is not provoked, thinks no evil; does not rejoice in iniquity, but rejoices in the truth; bears all things, believes all things, hopes all things, endures all things" (1 Corinthians 13:4-7).

Unity, liberty, and charity. God grant us the wisdom to know the difference between matters of faith and opinion and when to exercise unity and liberty! One way to tell the difference is consistency. The word of God does not contradict. If we have reached a conclusion or an opinion that is contradictory, then we must recognize it is not from God, go back to the drawing board, and reconsider our conviction. Moreover, God's will and word will always be good, right, and true (Ephesians 5:9). It will always be all three, never just one or two. If our conviction is not good, right, *and* true, then it is not the will and word of God. It is time to reconsider.

If we teach and practice these maxims in our approach to the scriptures and one another, we will be faithful to God. If we ignore these maxims in our approach to the scriptures, we will inevitably return to the religious error and bondage from which our forefathers broke free.

What are they hearing in the church? If they are hearing the preacher give more than or less than the word of God – speaking where God has not spoken – a great evil is occurring. If they are hearing manmade creeds and opinions in addition to the word of God, they will be divided. If they are not hearing the virtues of faith, unity, forbearance in opinions, and love, they will eventually cease to exist as a congregation of the Lord's people. If the preacher truly desires to edify the body of Christ, and save those who hear him, he will stick to preaching the gospel, in season and out of season. The last thing the church needs to happen is for the preacher to overstep his bounds and become judge, jury, and executioner.

Continue in Them

"Take heed to yourself and unto the doctrine" or "teachings" and "continue in them." If he is truly to take heed to the teachings of Christ and His holy apostles, the minister of Christ must continue in them. Paul also encouraged Timothy to "wage the good warfare" (1 Timothy 1:18) and "fight the good fight of faith" (1 Timothy 6:12).

The church is at war with Satanic forces of evil. To say that the church is at war with false teachers and the false doctrines they teach is no understatement. "For though we walk in the flesh, we do not war according to the flesh. For the weapons of our warfare are not carnal but mighty in God for pulling down strongholds, casting down arguments and every high thing that exalts itself against the knowledge of God, bringing every thought into captivity to the obedience of Christ, and being ready to punish all disobedience when your obedience is fulfilled" (2 Corinthians 10:3-6). If ever there was a time for ministers of the gospel to continue steadfastly in the teachings of the gospel, that time surely is now.

Jude was inspired to address this need as well. God wanted His people to know the importance of contending earnestly for the faith (Jude 3). To contend literally means to fight in defense of something. God, through His servant Jude, was teaching us that our faith, the faith which is in Christ Jesus, is worth fighting to protect. As Paul said, it is not a carnal or physical war that is being waged, but a spiritual war, a war of knowledge between good and evil, between obedience and disobedience. To win this war against the forces of darkness, God's people must first know their enemy. Anyone willing to walk after the works of the flesh and not the will of God is an enemy of the cross of Christ, whether they realize it or not.

Paul wrote, "Brethren, join in following my example, and note those who so walk, as you have us for a pattern. For many walk, of whom I have told you often, and now tell you even weeping, that they are the enemies of the cross of Christ: whose end is destruction, whose god is their belly, and whose glory is in their shame who set their mind on earthly things" (Philippians 3:17-19).

So that we might know the enemy and what to expect of them, Jude gives us several descriptions. Beginning in verse four, Jude writes, "For certain men have crept in unnoticed, who long ago were marked out for this condemnation, ungodly men, who turn the grace of our God into licentiousness and deny the only Lord God and our Lord Jesus Christ." You will observe that these "ungodly men" crept in unnoticed. Having crept in, and perhaps having gained a foothold, they began promoting their Satanic agenda of defiling the flesh, rejecting authority, and speaking evil of glories or "glorious ones" (Jude 8). They "speak evil of whatever they do not know; and whatever they know naturally, like brute beasts, in these things they corrupt themselves" (Jude 10).

Jude continued by describing them as "spots in your love feasts, while they feast with you without fear, serving only themselves; they are clouds without water, carried about by the winds; late autumn trees without fruit, twice dead, pulled up by the roots; raging waves of the sea, foaming up their own shame; wandering stars for whom is reserved the blackness of darkness forever" (Jude 12-13).

Doubtless, these false teachers are "ungodly sinners" committing "ungodly deeds...in an ungodly way," speaking "harsh things" against the Christ who shall ultimately bring His victorious judgment against them (Jude 15). Jude's inspired description of these ungodly men continues: "These are murmurers, complainers, walking according to their own lusts; and they mouth great swelling words, flattering people to gain advantage" (Jude 16). Having read that verse, you will observe that another one of their methods is to flatter people to gain advantage – not to encourage, not to teach, not to love – but solely for the advancement of their devilish schemes and "ungodly lusts" (Jude 18). They are "mockers...sensual persons, who cause divisions, not having the Spirit" (Jude 19).

For the Lord's people to win this war, not only must we know the enemy we face, but we must "remember the words which were spoken before by the apostles of our Lord Jesus Christ...building yourselves up on your most holy faith, praying in the Holy Spirit...keep yourselves in the love of God, looking for the mercy of our Lord Jesus Christ unto eternal life. And on some have compassion, making a distinction; but others save with fear, pulling them out of the fire, hating even the garment defiled by the flesh" (Jude 17-23).

Herein Jude gives us seven admonitions to secure victory against the ungodly enemy we face: (1) Keep in memory the teachings of scripture; (2) Keep building your faith; (3) Keep praying in the Spirit; (4) Keep yourselves in the love of God; (5) Keep looking for the mercy of Christ that will lead to life eternal; (6) Keep saving souls – whether by compassion or fear; (7) Keep hating the works of the flesh which defile the precious souls Christ came to save.

When we practice these seven principles we will be earnestly contending for the faith once delivered, exposing the enemies of God and their satanic agenda to destroy the church, while continuing to win souls for Christ by keeping His precious mission alive and well.

Jude teaches us that as Christians, it is our job to expose these creeping and ungodly men for what they are and what they are trying to accomplish, comparing their devilish deeds to the true grace, mercy, and teachings of Christ Jesus. As God's servants, let us gratefully and sincerely appreciate all that He is willing to do for us. Let us live according to the teachings of the Holy Spirit, while faithfully and accurately depicting the glorious Christ in an ungodly world. "Now to Him who is able to keep you from stumbling, and to present you faultless before the presence of His glory with exceeding joy, to God our Savior, who alone is wise, be glory and majesty, dominion and power, both now and forever. Amen" (Jude 24-25).

Those Who Hear You - 1 Timothy 4:16

As we come to the third and final portion of our study, we shall concern ourselves with the people to whom we minister as preachers of the gospel. We will divide the adherents of our message into three groups – the church, the home, and the community. The goal of the preacher's ministry must be kept ever before him – to "save those who hear you."

Preaching is not a popularity contest, for what is right is not always popular and what is popular is not always right. Success is not always determined by longevity and certainly not through one's fiscal earnings. The only question that matters when considering the success or failure of a ministry is whether the man of God helped (or did his best to help) the people who heard him better their relationship with God.

Ministry in the Church

Turning our attention to practical matters of ministry in a congregation, it goes without saying, but some of the minister's greatest friends and deepest disappointments will come from those in his congregation. For every Luke there is a Demas. Such is the nature of the relationship between the preacher and the church. Not everyone is going to like the preacher. Not everyone is going to be honest with the preacher. Even Jesus has His Judas. Yet, for the cause of Christ, the work must go on, and the faithful minister must press forward in his high calling.

A preacher's leadership is limited. He is not an overseer (elder, pastor, shepherd). He can only encourage through his personal relationship with the congregation, through his sermons and classes, and by example. One of his challenges in this setting is to help his elders become greater spiritual leaders and avoid becoming managers, without appearing to be managing them. An organization can outgrow its leadership. Leaders should view their opportunity to lead in a spiritually minded way, to be spiritual giants and to lead the people with the shared purpose and vision of saving souls and going to heaven.

Leadership requires letting others know what the goal is and then entrusting them with the responsibility to achieve that goal by utilizing their unique talents and abilities, while helping the entire congregation grow spiritually and enjoy greater spiritual mindedness.

To facilitate spiritual growth, we must recognize that "to be carnally minded is death, but to be spiritually minded is life and peace" (Romans 8:6). The spiritual man:

➢ Delights in the law of God (Romans 7:22).

➢ Serves the law of God (Romans 7:25).

➢ Has a mind which is set on spiritual things (Romans 8:5).

To be spiritually minded is life and peace. It is to set one's affections on the heaven that awaits him and the good that he can do by being trained and disciplined to view the world as God views it. God is speaking to the inner man, that which is made in His likeness, and He is teaching us to view the world as He views it; to see sin as He sees it; to love as He loves; and to trust in Him for life and peace.

As leaders of God people, we should desire a *true* spiritual conversion among God's people. It is all too easy to keep one foot in the world and one foot in the kingdom. Many of us still love to dabble in sin. The cross is somewhere inside of us, but it is not centermost, it is not utmost. We have a need for revival, and it must be a revival of the mind, of the will of man.

In helping to lead the congregation in their spiritual development, we should wish for them to learn that the mind is the primary instrument with which we glorify God. If the battle for the mind is lost, we will have lost our ability to glorify God. A mind that is not spiritual can never worship God in spirit (John 4:23-24). A mind that is not spiritual can never practice personal holiness – "For those who live according to the flesh set their minds on the things of the flesh, but those who live according to the Spirit, the things of the Spirit" (Romans 8:5). A mind that is not spiritual can never obey the Lord, and thus please the Lord – "Because the carnal mind is enmity against God; for it is not subject to the law of God, nor indeed can be. So then, those who are in the flesh cannot please God" (Romans 8:7-8). A mind that is not set on spiritual things can never win souls for the Lord (Luke 22:31-32). Truly, as a man thinks in his heart so is he (Proverbs 23:7).

The mind can either bask in light or abide in darkness; but light and darkness cannot co-exist. Our understanding can be darkened; or we can walk in light. We can either allow the carnal things of the world to overcome us; or we can overcome the world through Christ. In the darkness, you will find the evil things and thoughts of the world. This mind is enmity with God. In the light you will find wisdom that "is first pure, then peaceable, gentle, and easy to be entreated, full of mercy, and good fruits, without partiality, and without hypocrisy. And the fruit of righteousness is sown in peace of them that make peace" (James 3:17-18).

In attempting to help in the spiritual formation of the congregation, the preacher gauges their fruit of the Spirit (Galatians 5:22-26). The spiritually minded church manifests their spirituality in this way, crucifying (sacrificing) the passions and desires of the flesh. To walk in the Spirit is to live the life God has always intended us to live. However, to fulfill the lust of the flesh (Galatians 5:19-21) is to be everything contrary to God's will for our lives.

A great challenge for preachers in the present day is to revive spirituality amid a society which loves to be entertained. Sports have become a god to many Christians. Church services are missed with little to no thought, but hundreds of miles will be driven to make a sporting event. Our priorities are askew; and this indoctrination of worldliness has led to two great problems among God's people – ignorance and arrogance. We are ignorant of God's will and arrogant in our own conceitedness. We don't know God and we don't care. We are ignorant and arrogant. This sinful attitude has led many of us to question the relevance of the gospel and the church.

The challenges of worldliness, ignorance, and arrogance are manifested any time the goals of increased spiritual mindedness and spiritual formation are to be achieved. Man must be renewed in the spirit of his mind (Ephesians 4:23-24). He must be strengthened in his inner man (Ephesians 3:16). He must forsake the world, the course of the world, and cease being a man of the world.

The character, the attitude of the mind, must be changed/renewed. Once the character (the spirit of the mind) is renewed, everything else will fall into place. If the character of the mind is not changed, the person will never be truly and completely Christian. The Christian cannot continue thinking as a man of the world and expect to live a new life. If we desire a genuine religion we must have a genuine change of attitude, character, and will. Thus, the genuineness of our conversion will be seen in the life we live and in the life of the church.

Without the renewing of the mind, some of us will never become or remain Christians. Here you have the explanation for hypocrisy in the church. With the renewing of the mind, man can break the hold the devil has on him. Man can move forward and grow as God would have him to grow. Man can begin to view life and to experience life as God would have it.

The minister must seek to motivate the congregation to accept and apply the goal of spiritual growth. Some are best motivated by fear, I suppose (cf. Ecclesiastes 12:13; Jude 22-23). Others are motivated by the thought of reward (cf. Revelation 22:12, 14). While these are tremendous biblical forms of motivation, yet the greatest of these is love. Love for God can certainly motivate us to obey the Lord (cf. John 14:15). If we will only seek to understand the cross and the great love and mercy of God (Ephesians 2:4ff.), we will find all the motivation we need to forsake and denounce sin, and to live according to the gospel of grace and truth.

Paul found his motivation in the cross. "But God forbid that I should boast except in the cross of our Lord Jesus Christ, by whom the world has been crucified to me, and I to the world" (Galatians 6:14). The apostle Paul had plenty of things about which he could boast. He noted, "though I also might have confidence in the flesh. If anyone else thinks he may have confidence in the flesh, I more so: circumcised the eighth day, of the stock of Israel, of the tribe of Benjamin, a Hebrew of the Hebrews; concerning the law, a Pharisee; concerning zeal, persecuting the church; concerning the righteousness which is in the law, blameless" (Philippians 3:4-6). Yet, when he compared these things to the cross, they became utterly worthless.

He reasoned, "But what things were gain to me, these I have counted loss for Christ. Yet indeed I also count all things loss for the excellence of the knowledge of Christ Jesus my Lord, for whom I have suffered the loss of all things, and count them as rubbish, that I may gain Christ and be found in Him, not having my own righteousness, which is from the law, but that which is through faith in Christ, the righteousness which is from God by faith; that I may know Him and the power of His resurrection, and the fellowship of His sufferings, being conformed to His death, if, by any means, I may attain to the resurrection from the dead" (vv.7-10).

Paul was a changed man. The cross changed him. The cross taught him how to live, how to sacrifice, how to suffer, and how to die. He could not boast in the law. The law could not save. The law only exposed him to be a sinner. He could not boast in his morality. He could not boast in his self-sufficiency. He was in sin and dead to God. Paul could only boast in the cross of our Lord Jesus Christ. Only in the cross could he find redemption. Only in the cross could he find forgiveness. Only in the cross could he find hope. Only in the cross could he find life and peace.

For Paul, to glory in the cross was to glory in the redeeming, sanctifying work of God. The cross meant everything to him. He placed all of his trust in it and devoted his life to preaching it. To glory in the cross is to glory in the power of God. "For the message of the cross is foolishness to those who are perishing, but to us who are being saved it is the power of God" (1 Corinthians 1:18).

It is because Paul valued the love of God and revered His power that he could say, "...by whom the world has been crucified to me, and I to the world." Again, "For the love of Christ compels us, because we judge thus: that if One died for all, then all died; and He died for all, that those who live should live no longer for themselves, but for Him who died for them and rose again" (2 Corinthians 5:14-15).

Paul surrendered his life to Christ. "And those who are Christ's have crucified the flesh with its passions and desires" (Galatians 5:24). Paul could not turn his back on the cross – it meant too much to him! The world no longer held any great attraction to Paul. For him, "To live is Christ and to die is gain" (Philippians 1:21). Paul was a man who desired above all else to go home and be with his Lord. He did not glory in this world's possessions, attainments, or gratifications. He gloried only in the cross of Christ. He did not feel attached to this world any more except that he might win others to Christ. The world was crucified to him and he was crucified to the world.

It is a great challenge to be in the world and yet not of the world. It may be difficult, but it is absolutely good, and true, and right. "For the grace of God that brings salvation has appeared to all men, teaching us that, denying ungodliness and worldly lusts, we should live soberly, righteously, and godly in the present age, looking for the blessed hope and glorious appearing of our great God and Savior Jesus Christ, who gave Himself for us, that He might redeem us from every lawless deed and purify for Himself His own special people, zealous for good works" (Titus 2:11-14).

The man of God is not intended to resemble the man of the world. The man of God is altogether different. This is because of the cross. The man of God glories in the cross because the blood that was shed on it purchased his redemption, his church, his gospel, and his heavenly home. The man of the world cares very little for these things. His mind is set on carnal things. Our minds are set on heavenly things.

How can this challenge become not so challenging? As ministers, we must help our congregations look to the cross; thus "looking unto Jesus, the author and finisher of our faith, who for the joy that was set before Him endured the cross, despising the shame, and has sat down at the right hand of the throne of God. For consider Him who endured such hostility from sinners against Himself, lest you become weary and discouraged in your souls" (Hebrews 12:2-3)

We must help them to live for the cross, for Him "who Himself bore our sins in His own body on the tree, that we, having died to sins, might live for righteousness—by whose stripes you were healed. For you were like sheep going astray, but have now returned to the Shepherd and Overseer of your souls" (1 Peter 2:24-25). And we must help them to love the cross. "How I love that old cross where the dearest and best for a world of lost sinners was slain." We cannot truly know Jesus until we know Him as the crucified Savior of the world. We must know Him as our Savior and glory in the cross.

Let us not be anxious to set timelines for the spiritual growth and development of the church. Realize that we all grow at different levels and are at different levels of spiritual maturity even now. Spiritual growth takes time, but the harvest is worth the wait. Look for various indications of spiritual growth, such as worship and Bible study attendance, participation in the various ministries of the church, and primarily the outlook and attitude of everyone in general. Help them grown from within, from the inner man. If the church grows spiritually, it will inevitably grow numerically.

Desire for this church to be a God-honoring, God-glorifying congregation. Everything you hope to accomplish in the church depends upon whether you can help them to glory in the cross. Through the cross, we will come to know God, love God, and grow in God. If we will grow spiritually into the image of our dear Lord, we will inevitably grow numerically. Numerical growth is a fruit born by those who have first grown spiritually.

Spiritual mindedness will cause one to see the importance of honoring God. The spiritually minded man is going to see God for who He truly is and glorify Him for it (see Hebrews 12:26-28). He is going to recognize the cross for what it truly means and honor Christ for it. He is going to see the Bible for what it truly is and receive the Spirit from it. He is going to see himself as he truly is and turn to God for salvation.

Spiritual mindedness will also cause one to see the importance of preparing for eternity. The carnally minded man scoffs at eternity and dismisses all that the Lord has taught. The spiritually minded man accepts that he has an immortal soul and that he will live somewhere forever. We have one opportunity to live this life. The spiritually minded man will enjoy all the blessings God gives in this life, but he will never become overly attached to the world. He knows there is a better home awaiting him. He not only longs for that home, but he desires to help others realize it as well.

The preacher's plans and goals shouldn't center upon new buildings or increased budgets, but one goal – the spiritual growth and maturity of the church he serves. To help them achieve this goal he must also grow spiritually, and he must use his opportunity as a minister of the gospel to encourage them. He must place the cross in the center of his heart so that it will be in the center of his preaching. May the cross be in the center of everything we do for His honor and glory.

When the preacher is spiritually minded, working alongside elders who are spiritually minded, and serving a congregation that is spiritually minded, the ministry will most likely have longevity, fruitful labors, love, unity, and joy. All the incidentals to the ministry will take care of themselves. Evil will be overcome with good, fellowship will be sweet, friendships will endure, and souls will be saved. What more could a preacher ask for than that?

Ministry in the Home

The home is the oldest institution given by God and second only in importance to the church. Those who have been blessed by a Christian home can affirm that God knew what He was doing when He gave us the home. As goes the home, so goes society. Psalm 127:1 can apply to any institution, but it especially applies to the home. "Unless the Lord builds the house, they labor in vain who build it."

One might consider Noah to have been a failure at preaching. After all, he preached for 120 years and only saved eight souls, including his own. But those seven people he convinced to enter the Ark were his family. As ministers we must take heed to ourselves, making our calling and election sure, and of no less importance, we must take heed to our families.

Many ministers have had their ministry undone by their unruly children. Children often are what parents allow them to be. One case which verifies this statement is found in 1 Samuel, and it is the case of Eli and his two sons, Phinehas and Hophni. Eli was rebuked by God for not restraining his sons as they executed their priestly duties in a sinful way. We know that Eli talked to his sons about their wickedness, but he did not stop them from continuing in their wickedness. Eli stopped at words. In so doing, he allowed his sons to continue sinning against God (see 1 Samuel 2:29ff.). It is good to talk with our children, but sometimes action is required.

Moreover, children are often what you expect them to be. Have high expectations for your children! Expect them to be faithful Christians. Expect them to be outstanding citizens. Expect them to excel in the classroom and/or workplace. Let them know that these things are expected. It is troubling to see many Christian parents settle for "good kids" (as the world deems goodness) who have very loose morals. If you expect nothing of a child, you will get nothing from a child.

Lastly, children are what you train them to be. It is not enough to have great expectations for our children; we must also take an active part in their training. As parents, we must provide them with the tools, opportunities, and training to be successful in life. Preachers must be active in the lives of their children. Know where your children are, what they are doing, and share your lives with them. Prepare your children for the world, rather than simply turning them loose on the world! "Train up a child in the way he should go." And "bring them up in the nurture and admonition of the Lord." This kind of parenting involves both nurturing and correcting.

Many parents are sold on the idea of nurturing their children, while they give very little credence to the principle of correcting them. The Bible tells us that if you do not correct your children, essentially, you hate them. "He who spares his rod hates his son, But he who loves him disciplines him promptly" (Proverbs 13:24). "Chasten your son while there is hope" (Proverbs 19:18); for "Foolishness is bound up in the heart of a child; but the rod of correction will drive it far from him" (Proverbs 22:15).

Yet, let us not overlook the vital importance of nurturing our children in the Lord. Children must learn the importance of sound instruction, wisdom, mercy, forgiveness, kindness, righteousness, work ethic, love for family, love for the Lord, and love for mankind. As a child observes these qualities in his parents and learns these truths from childhood, he is nurtured in the Lord.

The greatest legacy any preacher will ever leave is his children; and the greatest thing you will ever do for your child is to bring them to Christ. Perhaps the greatest hope we have for the children in this country is for Christian parents to raise their children in such a way as not to be affected by evil environments, but to affect their environments for good, for Christ, and His gospel. Let us train them to meet the devil *on the Lord's terms* and help them to build a faith that will lead them to victory. May God be able to say of his preacher the things he said of Abraham long ago: "For I have known him, in order that he may command his children and his household after him, that they keep the way of the Lord, to do righteousness and justice."

Obviously, this type of parenting will be much easier when the preacher and his wife are working together with these everlasting goals in mind. A man and his wife must determine what kind of life they are going to build together before they begin building. Once they begin, they need to stick to the blueprint. It would be silly to begin building a house and not follow the blueprint, but it would be tragic to begin building a Christian home and stray from the plans.

A preacher's wife must learn to live in a glass house. It's not fair, it's just the way it is. Your home must be open to guests, and if necessary, provide a place for someone to eat and sleep. Sacrifices will be made of your time, your husband, and your energy. Preparations for Sunday will often need to be made on Saturday. Sunday dinner will include your family and whoever your husband happened to invite. Gospel preachers may stay in your home like stray cats, sharing stories until well past bedtime.

In addition to these inconveniences, she must deal with the serious matter of her husband's moods. He will feel inadequate often. She will console him. He will be depressed at the progress of his work. She will encourage him. He will preach a "dud" of a sermon and she will speak of the positives of what he had to say. He will make mistakes and she will help him to learn from them. He will stress over the family's finances, perhaps while going without pay raises, or benefits, and she will make do.

Some women will balk at the idea of being a preacher's wife. But those blessed women who have lived it have a treasure-trove of memories and blessings to share. The man of God could not do his work without the woman of God. Ministry truly is a team effort between the husband and the wife.

As with unruly children, some preachers have wives who are detrimental to their ministry. Some women are not suited simply because they are not spiritually minded enough to endure what may be required of them. It is no small thing to be a preacher's wife. It can be demanding and cruel. The women who endure do so not only because they love their husbands, but they love the Lord with all their being. They realize the importance of the work they are doing together. They withstand the criticisms and endure the loneliness of a husband who is gone off preaching somewhere, while caring for their children, their homes, and often working a secular job. "A woman who fears the Lord shall be praised." Praise her often, shower her with affection, for if you have such a wife as this you need not to be told "her worth is far above rubies."

Ministry in the Community

A preacher may experience culture shock in some communities where he is called to labor. A young man may be reared in a small country town, study at university, and then receive a call to move to a large metropolis and preach for a city congregation. Another preacher may have the exact opposite experience. He may move to a small town after living in an urban environment his entire life. A man from the southern states may move north. Or one from the east may move west. Any preacher who has experienced such a move can attest to the fact that some communities, like personalities, are vastly different from others. Yet, one thing remains the same – man's need for Christ.

Regardless of where or when the preacher may go, he will encounter souls in societies facing a spiritual crisis. Especially is this true in America. "Oh, thou America, what is thy reaping? Oh, while hell is astir, thou art still sleeping!" One needs only to look at the nations chronicled in scripture to find sufficient warning for the present day.

The Nations and Their Rebellions

- Sodom and Gomorrah – homosexuality

- Ammon – cruelty, covetousness, and greed

- Moab – pride and hatred for God's people

- Edom – pride and hatred for God's people

- Tyre – pride and boasting of its beauty

- Philistia – idolatry

- Phoenicia – idolatry; child sacrifices

- Assyria – excessive cruelty

- Media – pride and cruelty

- Egypt – idolatry and material pleasure

- Babylon – idolatry and wealth

- Israel and Judah – apostasy and hypocrisy

- Rome – wickedness, pride, and power

Each of these nations shared in a general rejection of God and each of these sins eerily resembles our Western society.

God's Response to the Nations

- God destroyed nations when He saw they were no longer fit to continue (Genesis 15:12-16; Amos 2:9-10).

- He destroyed nations for persistent sin without repentance – "For three transgressions and for four" (Amos 1-2).

- God would not stand the sin of these nations forever; "I am weighed down by you" (Amos 2:13; 3:2).

- God would not destroy a nation for the sake of the righteous in it (Gen. 18:22ff.).

- God would not destroy a nation if they repented (Jonah/ Nineveh; Jer. 18:7-10).

- God did not destroy any of them without ample time to repent (multiple prophets warned them; Amos 2:11-12; 2 Peter 3:9).

- Yet, there came a time when God would not stand their sin anymore (cf. Gen. 6:5-7).

America's Rebellion to God

- Violent Crimes – 1,203,808 violent crimes occurred nationwide in 2019; 3,300 per day.[1]

- Abortions – 862,320 in the US in 2017.

- Overdoses – 70,630 in 2019.

- Suicide – In 2019 suicide was the tenth leading cause of death overall in the United States, claiming the lives of over 47,500 people.

- LGBTQ – In 2001, 53 percent of respondents to a survey stated they believed gay or lesbian relations to be morally wrong, but in 2020 this number had fallen to 32 percent.

- All the while, Americans are becoming increasingly prideful, powerful, materially rich, and yet, spiritually bankrupt.

In our nation there is a movement not only to reject God, but to erase and eradicate Him. How will God respond to this nation? The answer depends on us. We are the 10 righteous souls (Genesis 18:32). If we ever give up or give in, then what would prevent God from removing this nation like He has so many others? Revival is

---

[1] We decided to use pre-Covid 19 stats as the riots of 2020 could skew the trends we are seeing.

critical to the survival and future of this country. Without faithful gospel preachers encouraging Christians to initiate revival, this country has a perilous future at best.

The world will not always agree with the gospel preacher, and the faithful preacher is not going to be the most popular citizen in town. He may never receive the key to city, but he can have an influence for lasting good upon those "within the limits of the sphere which God appointed" (2 Corinthians 10:13).

A preacher can widen his sphere of influence by doing business with those in his community. Home maintenance, local businesses, restaurants, and in-person communication with those who sell insurance, realtors, bankers, etc., will help to increase his friends and acquaintances in the town. If all his business transactions are done online, opportunities to meet people will be greatly diminished. Friends and family members of the church will also help to build a sizeable list of prospective adherents to the gospel.

Depending on the schools and school board in the community, a preacher and his wife may want to consider homeschooling. It would certainly be wiser to homeschool a child and forgo a few relationships than to subject them to drag shows and the like. A minister of the gospel is not to "suffer fools gladly." If a good Christian school is available in the community, it could be a great place to build relationships.

If the preacher is moving into a community that has many churches of like precious faith, he should seek to build relationships with fellow Christians and preachers from other congregations. Avoid competing with them for members. The devil is the only one we should be competing against. An abundant number of churches in an area will cause some members to change their membership from church to church all too often. Sometimes it is justified and sometimes it is not. If hurt and harm has occurred, help them to reconcile and return to their home congregation. Sheep stealing will only cause hard feelings among sister congregations. However, if a soul is wayward, that soul must be restored, regardless of past affiliations. The preacher (and every Christian) is obligated to "convert the sinner from the error of his way" and "save a soul from death."

As we consider our communities, let us seek to bring them to Christ one soul at a time. Remain ever looking for one more soul to save. The future of that community may very well be changed for good through the influence of *one* man bringing a message from God, just as was the case with Jonah and Nineveh. When your soul faints within you, remember the Lord, and go to work (Jonah 2:7).

Salvation: The Heart of the Matter

"Take heed to yourself and to the doctrine. Continue in them, for in doing this you will save both yourself and those who hear you" (1 Timothy 4:16). At the heart of Paul's charge to Timothy is salvation, salvation for the preacher and for the flock. Nothing else matters if the soul is lost. Multimillion-dollar buildings and million-dollar budgets will be of no avail on the day of judgment if the souls of the preacher and the congregation are not right with God. A minister would be better off to preach in a small, country church with few people where he is unimpeded to preach the whole counsel of God than to be in a metropolitan setting with thousands of people and yet find himself restricted in his sacred duty.

No amount of salary, prestige, or perks compares to the value of the soul. "What shall it profit a man" if he gains all these things and loses his own soul. A man must know he is ultimately accountable to God for his preaching ministry and keep the day of reckoning ever before him as he prepares and presents his message. Otherwise, he risks becoming nothing more than hireling who will, through his covetousness, deceive others with empty words, fair speeches, and vain promises.

Let the gospel preacher aspire to be a man of conviction, a man of God. Whether he is ministering in a large or small church, let him obey God and "preach to it the message that I tell you" (Jonah 3:2). May he have truly spiritual goals and reach them through "Him who is able to make you stand." Only by being a faithful preacher of the gospel will genuine spiritually be attained. May he survey the wondrous cross on which the Prince of glory died, and pour contempt on all his pride. The ministry of the word has never been about being the biggest or the best, but being faithful to Him who called you. With these thoughts in mind, we shall conclude our little study of 1 Timothy 4:16. May God richly bless all those seeking to keep the mission of Christ alive by preaching the glorious gospel of salvation to a lost and dying world.

Appendix

Preparing the Man, the Ministry, and the Message
from the Pastoral Epistles

Introduction

I.   Paul's Relationship with Timothy and Titus

    A. Relationship building will be important to your ministry and to the preparation of other ministers.

    B. Paul was a mentor to Timothy and Titus and regarded them as "sons" in the faith (1 Tim. 1:2; Titus 1:4).

II.   The Pastoral Epistles helped to prepare Timothy and Titus as men, in their ministries, and with their messages.

Discussion

I.   Preparing the Man

    A. Mindset

        1.) Fight as a soldier (1 Tim. 1:18; 1 Tim. 6:12; 2 Tim. 2:3; 2 Tim. 4:7).

        2.) Have a clean conscience (1 Tim. 1:19).

        3.) Keep a spirit of power, love, and a sound mind (2 Tim. 1:7).

        4.) Be gentle, patient, humble (2 Tim. 2:24).

    B. Work Ethic

        1.) Do not neglect the gift, favor, grace (1 Tim. 4:14).

        2.) Be diligent (2 Tim. 2:15).

        3.) Do the work of an evangelist (2 Tim. 4:5).

C. Endurance

    1.) Labor and suffer reproach (1 Tim. 4:10).

    2.) Hold fast (2 Tim. 1:13).

    3.) Endure hardship and afflictions (2 Tim. 2:3; 4:5).

D. Flee/Avoid/Reject

    1.) Flee these things (love of money, covetousness) (1 Tim. 6:11).

    2.) Avoid babblings and contradictions of false knowledge (1 Tim. 6:20; 2 Tim. 2:16).

    3.) Flee youthful lusts (2 Tim. 2:22).

    4.) Avoid foolish and ignorant disputes (2 Tim. 2:23; Titus 3:9).

    5.) Reject a divisive man (Titus 3:10-11).

E. Pursue/Follow

    1.) Pursue righteousness, godliness, faith, love, patience, gentleness, and peace (1 Tim. 6:11-12; 2 Tim. 2:22).

    2.) Follow Paul's doctrine, manner of life, purpose, faith, longsuffering, etc. (2 Tim. 3:10).

        a.) Here we have mentoring exemplified by Paul.

        b.) "You must continue…" (2 Tim. 3:14).

        c.) "Commit to faithful men…" (2 Tim. 2:2).

F. Example

    1.) Be an example to believers in word, conduct, love, spirit, faith, and purity (1 Tim. 4:12).

2.) In all things show yourself to be a pattern for good works (Titus 2:7-8).

II.   Preparing the Ministry

A. Part of the work of ministry is to set in order what is lacking/needed (Titus 1:5).

  1.) What is most needed?

  2.) What is the desired goal?

  3.) What kind of preaching and teaching is required to accomplish the goal?

B. In ministry we must answer false doctrines and teachers (1 Tim. 1:3-4).

  1.) Identify them (1 Tim. 4:1-3; 2 Tim. 3:1ff.; 2 Tim. 3:13).

  2.) Answer them (Titus 1:9-11).

  3.) Reject them (Titus 3:10-11).

C. Teach sound doctrine (Titus 2:1).

  1.) Sound doctrine can only come from the inspired word of God (2 Tim. 3:16-17).

  2.) This word must be preached (2 Tim. 4:1ff.).

  3.) Only when we preach the word, can we speak with all authority (Titus 2:15).

D. Be a good minister (1 Tim. 4:6).

  1.) Do the work of an evangelist and fulfill your ministry (2 Tim. 4:5).

  2.) Affirm constantly that brethren must continue in good works (Titus 3:8).

3.) Give yourself entirely to the work (1 Tim. 4:15).

E. Understand relationship and gender dynamics in ministry.

    1.) Women, widows (1 Timothy 2:8ff.; 1 Tim. 5:3ff.; Titus 2:3-5).

    2.) Men – young and old (1 Tim. 5:1ff; Titus 2:1-2, 6-8).

F. See to the establishment and maintaining of biblical leadership in the churches.

    1.) Elders (1 Tim. 3:1-7; 1 Tim. 5:17-25; Titus 1:5-9)

    2.) Deacons (1 Tim. 3:8-13).

    3.) Preachers (2 Tim. 2:2).

III. Preparing the Message

A. Preaching must have a purpose.

    1.) Bring to light life and immortality through the gospel (2 Tim. 1:10).

    2.) Give attention to reading, exhortation, and doctrine (1 Tim. 4:13).

    3.) Powerful verbs – charge, remind, command, correct, etc.

B. Three Essentials for Great Preaching

    1.) Know the word (2 Tim. 2:15; 2 Tim. 3:15).

    2.) Know the people (1 Tim. 1:3-4; Titus 1:12-13).

    3.) Have the courage to make the connection from the pulpit to the pew (2 Tim. 1:7-8).

C. Each sermon should state the truth, correct error intended to contradict the truth, and exhort the hearer to obey the truth. Convince, rebuke, and exhort (2 Tim. 4:2).

Conclusion

I.   The importance of biblical preaching cannot be overstated.

   A. Every great religious revival has had at its heart great preaching.

   B. Every great congregation has been built up by great preaching.

II.   There is no substitute for biblical preaching.

   A. The place of preaching in the church can never be replaced or substituted.

   B. The place of faithful preachers can never be replaced or substituted in the church.

III.   From the Pastoral Epistles (1, 2 Timothy and Titus), we have studied the preparation of the man, the ministry, and the message.

   A. Preparing the message (homiletics) is the easiest of the three.

   B. To prepare the ministry faithfully, one must give himself entirely to it for many years.

   C. To prepare the man, one must give himself entirely to it for the remainder of his life.

   D. Are you willing to prepare yourself for ministry in the Lord's church?

Bibliography

Baxter, Batsell Barrett. *The Heart of the Yale Lectures*. New York: Macmillan, 1954.

Brooks, Phillips. *Lectures on Preaching*. New York: E.P. Dutton and Co., 1877.

Brown, Jr., H.C. *A Quest for Reformation in Preaching*. Nashville: Broadman Press, 1968.

Cahill, Dennis M. *The Shape of Preaching*. Grand Rapids, MI: Baker, 2007.

Casey, Michael W. *Saddlebags, City Streets & Cyberspace*. Abilene, TX: ACU Press, 1995.

Castleberry, Otis. *They Heard Him Gladly*. Rosemead, CA: Old Paths Publishing, 1963.

Colson, Charles and Nancy Pearcey. *How Now Shall We Live?* Carol Stream, IL: Tyndale House Publishers, 1999.

Gorman, Michael J. *Elements of Biblical Exegesis*. Grand Rapids, MI: Baker, 2009.

Hall, John. *God's Word through Preaching*. Reprint. Grand Rapids, MI: Baker, 1979.

Hoyt, Arthur S. *The Preacher: His Person, Message, and Method*. New York: Hodder & Stoughton, 1909.

Jividen, Jimmy. *More than a Feeling*. Nashville: Gospel Advocate Company, 1999.

Logan, Jr., Samuel, T. (Editor). *The Preacher and Preaching*. Phillipsburg, NJ: Presbyterian and Reformed Publishing Company, 1986.

Maclaren, Ian. *The Cure of Souls*. New York: Hodder &
    Stoughton, 1896.

Meyer, Jack Sr. *The Preacher and His Work*. Shreveport, LA:
    Lambert, 1960.

Morgan, G. Campbell. *Preaching*. (Reprint) Grand Rapids, MI:
    Baker, 1974.

Robinson, Haddon W. *Biblical Preaching*. Grand Rapids, MI:
    Baker Academic, 2001.

Spurgeon, Charles. *Spurgeon's Lectures to His Students*, ed.
    David Otis Fuller. Grand Rapids, MI: Zondervan, 1945.

Stott, John R.W. *Between Two Worlds*. Grand Rapids, MI:
    Eerdmans Publishing Company, 1982.

Taylor, William M. *The Ministry of the Word*. (Reprint) Grand
    Rapids, MI: Baker, 1975.

Wilburn, James. *The Hazard of the Die*. Malibu, CA: Pepperdine
    University Press.